DIRTY DANCING
IN AN ICE STORM
WITH THE X-MEN

and Other Fascinating Side Trips

Visit Locations Where Movies Were Filmed

The *You Can Go There*
Travel Series, Book 7

ABSOLUTELY AMAZING BOOKS

Manhanset House
Shelter Island Hts., New York 11965-0342

bricktower@aol.com • absolutelyamazingebooks.com

All rights reserved under the International and Pan-American Copyright Conventions. No part of this publication may be reproduced, stored in a retrieval system, or transmitted in any form or by any means, electronic, or otherwise, without the prior written permission of the copyright holder.
The Absolutely Amazing eBooks and Books colophons are trademarks of J. T. Colby & Company, Inc.

Library of Congress Cataloging-in-Publication Data
Rhoades, Shirrel
Dirty Dancing In An Ice Storm
p. cm.

1. TRAVEL / United States / General.
2. TRAVEL / Special Interest / Adventure.
3. TRAVEL / Special Interest / Hikes & Walks.
Nonfiction, I. Title.

ISBN: 978-1-955036-82-5, Trade Paper

Copyright © 2025 by Shirrel Rhoades.

December 2025

DIRTY DANCING
IN AN ICE STORM
WITH THE X-MEN

and Other Fascinating Side Trips

Visit Locations Where Movies Were Filmed

The *You Can Go There* Travel Series, Book 7

Shirrel Rhoades

Habent Sua Fata Libelli

THE YOU CAN GO THERE TRAVEL SERIES

By Shirrel Rhoades

Book One
*The Devil's Hop Yard
and Other Fascinating Side Trips*

Book Two
*Trapped in a Bahamian Cave
and Other Fascinating Side Trips*

Book Three
*Buried in Grant's Tomb
and Other Fascinating Side Trips*

Book Four
*Whispering in Grand Central Station
and Other Fascinating Side Trips*

Book Five
*Cracking the Da Vinci Code in Newport,
Finding a Secret Waterfall in Hawaii
and Other Fascinating Side Trips*

Book Six
*Dancing in the Aisles,
Drinking in the Chancel
and Other Fascinating Side Trips*

Book Seven
*Dirty Dancing in an Ice Storm
with the X-Men
and Other Fascinating Side Trips*

TABLE OF CONTENTS

Introduction..*1*

Chapter 1, *Dirty Dancing* *4*

Chapter 2, *It*..*12*

Chapter 3, *The Ice Storm*...*16*

Chapter 4, *A Christmas Story*..*22*

Chapter 5, *Cape Fear*..*28*

Chapter 6, *X-Men*..*35*

Chapter 7, *Fargo*..*40*

Chapter 8, *Being There*...*47*

Chapter 9, *Breaking Away*...*53*

Chapter 10, *A Place in the Sun*......................................*59*

Chapter 11, *The Hunger Games*....................................*65*

Chapter 12, *The Thomas Crown Affair*.........................*74*

Chapter 13, *The Sheik*...*82*

Chapter 14, *Star Wars: The Force Awakens*
                Star Wars: The Last Jedi........................*88*

Chapter 15, *The Great Gatsby*.......................................*95*

Chapter 16, *The Dark Knight Trilogy*..........................*104*

Chapter 17, *Midnight in Paris*..................................*112*

Chapter 18, *The Stepford Wives*..............................*119*

Chapter 19, *Jurassic Park*..*125*

Chapter 20, *Ghostbusters*.......................................*133*

Chapter 21, *The Shining*...*140*

Chapter 22, *La La Land*..*149*

Chapter 23, *The Lord of the Rings* Trilogy
               The Hobbit Trilogy..................*158*

Chapter 24, *James Bond* Films...............................*167*

Chapter 25, *The African Queen*..............................*174*

Chapter 26, *The Rose Tattoo*..................................*181*

Acknowledgments...*189*

About the Author..*191*

INTRODUCTION

The movie *Casablanca* (1942) was not filmed in Casablanca. Rather, it was shot entirely at Warner Bros. Studios in Burbank, California (except for one scene at Van Nuys Airport).

Three Billboards Outside Ebbing, Missouri (2017) was actually filmed in North Carolina. Matter of fact, there is no place called "Ebbing, Missouri."

The Dallas Buyer's Club (2013) was filmed in New Orleans instead of Dallas.

The Shawshank Redemption (1994) was set in Maine but filmed at the Mansfield Reformatory in Ohio.

While *Key Largo* (1948) is set in the Florida Keys, the film was primarily shot on a Warner Bros. sound stage in Hollywood, with only a few exterior shots filmed in the Florida Keys. The beach and hotel exterior were constructed on the studio's backlot; the interior scenes were filmed on a sound stage; and the boat scenes were filmed in Sound Stage 21, a huge indoor water tank.

There is a deliberate joke about this sort of thing in *The Kentucky Fried Movie*. We see an image of New York City and the Statue of Liberty, but a caption identifies it as being Hong Kong.

Several cities are frequently used as stand-ins for New York City in movies, particularly Toronto and Vancouver, due to their similar architecture and cost-effective production.

Films are often shot in locations that differ from the places where the story is set for practical reasons like cost, tax breaks, availability, or desired visual effects.

And some films are made entirely on a soundstage, with no outside locations at all.

One obvious example is *The Wizard of Oz* (1939). This classic film features colorful sets like the Yellow Brick Road and the Emerald City, all built on MGM soundstages.

Another is *2001: A Space Odyssey* (1968). Stanley Kubrick's sci-fi masterpiece utilized meticulously built sets for the spacecraft and space stations. After all, filming in space was not a viable option in '68.

Some films use a green screen to add the backdrop later (during post production). One production that used a green screen for just about everything was *Sky Captain and the World of*

Tomorrow (2004), a sci-fi fantasy where only the actors are real.

That said, most films use outside locations, real places that act as a stand-in for places required by the movie's plot.

Want to go there?

If you know where to look, you can personally visit many of these movie locations. You can walk in the footsteps of George Clooney, dance on the same street corner as Ryan Goslin and Emma Stone, sit on the bench made famous by Forrest Gump.

That's what this travel guide – another entry in the *You Can Go There* travel series – is about: places where movies were made that you can personally visit.

We recommend watching the respective films in advance, so you will be able to recognize these backdrops when you see them for real.

Shirrel Rhoades

CHAPTER 1
Dirty Dancing

About one mile from where I live is the site on Boys Camp Road where the movie *Dirty Dancing* was filmed. The boy's camp that substituted for the Catskills resort in the movie is long gone, replaced by Firefly Cove, a gated enclave of elegant homes surrounding a manorial clubhouse with a squarish blue pool, the deep green waters of Lake Lure, North Carolina, glittering in the background.

The clubhouse where much of the movie took place is now gone, only a stone wall still standing. You can't get inside the passcoded gate to see the wall, but you can get a good view if you drive past the gate, curving to your right on Chapel Point Road. You'll spot the ruins of the wall in the backyard of the first house on the passenger side.

While many of the exterior scenes for the fictional Kellerman's Resort were filmed at Mountain Lake Lodge in Pembroke, Virginia, the Lake Lure site provided the cabins and other familiar locales. I will focus on those, since I don't have to go far to show them off to friends.

A romantic drama, *Dirty Dancing* (1987) starred Jennifer Grey (daughter of Oscar-winner Joel Grey) and Patrick Swayze (son of dance instructor Patsy Karnes Swayze).

The movie has become a coming-of-age classic. You remember the ugly duckling story: Set in 1963, wallflower Frances "Baby" Houseman (Grey) falls for bad-boy dance instructor Johnny Castle (Swayze) at a posh Jewish vacation resort.

The famous quote – "Nobody puts Baby in a corner – ranks as #98 on American Film Institute's 100 Years ... 100 Quotes list.

Dirty Dancing's theme song – "(I've Had) The Time of My Life" – ranks as #86 on American Film Institute's 100 Years ... 100 Songs list. It won an Academy Award, a Golden Globe, and a Grammy.

And the film itself claims the #93 slot on American Film Institute's 100 Years ... 100 Passions list.

Dirty Dancing was directed by Emile Ardolino. He got the gig based on his Academy Award-winning documentary *He Makes Me Feel Like Dancing*. Openly gay, Ardolino had profiled dancers and choreographers for the PBS series *Dance in America* and *Live from Lincoln Center*. This was his first feature film.

Shot on a modest $6 million budget, *Dirty Dancing* earned over $214 million worldwide. It was also the first film to sell a million copies on video.

Although an iconic love story, it turns out that Jennifer Grey and Patrick Swayze did not get along off-screen. The clash stemmed from their previous work together on the movie *Red Dawn*. They had very different acting styles, with Swayze finding Grey unprofessional and Grey finding Swayze way too intense for her comfort.

I used to bump into Jennifer Grey (back when she was dating Matthew Broderick) at a small hole-in-the-wall eatery on Prince Street in the SoHo section of New York. It happened so frequently that we eventually began to nod our hellos to each other.

As for the famous lift in the movie, when Baby leaps into Johnny's outstretched hands, she had this to say: "I only did it on the day I shot it. Never rehearsed it, never done it since."

Of course, we see them practicing the leap while waist-deep in the lake. That was filmed just off today's Firefly Cove, although some claim it was shot in Virginia. Definitely, the dance on the log was shot in Lake Lure. And the stone stairway where Baby practiced her dance moves still stands and is easy to see in Firefly Cove.

The camp's gymnasium was transformed into the banquet room for the talent show and the final dance scene. As noted, the gym is now gone, but nearby Esmeralda Inn displays some of the original wood from the gymnasium. Unfortunately, Esmeralda is currently closed, a victim of Hurricane Helene which washed away the adjoining town of Chimney Rock in a catastrophic flash flood.

The golf scene where Baby asks her father for $250 was filmed on the 16th Hole of the Rumbling Bald Golf Course – a few streets over from where I live these days – on the backside of Lake Lure.

The 1927 Lake Lure Inn & Spa where the cast stayed during the filming of *Dirty Dancing* is still open for guests. On weekends you can join its patrons for a fabulous buffet Sunday Bruch. If you like, you can eat on the open-air Veranda, looking out on the Lake Lure Beach.

You can stay at Johnny's Cabin or Baby's Bungalow, both spacious *Dirty Dancing*-themed accommodations.

If you have time, stop off at the Lake Lure Marina at nearby Mead Park and take a boat tour. The guide will point out the house Patrick Swayze rented during the filming. Shirtless, he used to do his morning exercises atop the adjacent boathouse. He maintained his physical fitness through a combination of martial arts like Wushu, Taekwondo, and Aikido, integrating it with his dance background. Locals passed by on their motorized skiffs to wave at the Adonis-like figure. He would wave back, I'm told.

Swayze had formal dance training at the Harkness Ballet and Joffrey Ballet schools. Before playing Baby in *Dirty Dancing*, Jennifer Grey had very little to no prior dance experience – unlike her father who starred in *Cabaret*. But, as she points out, her character was a 17-year-old girl just learning to dance with the help of 25-year-old Johnny Castle.

Grey was in truth 27 when she did the movie. And Swayze was seven years older at 34.

~ ~ ~

You can relive the movie at the Kellerman's Resort Theme Weekend in Pembroke, Virginia. The resort hosts *Dirty Dancing*-themed weekends, and visitors can stay in the Virginia Cottage, where Baby and her family bunked in the film. There's a free map offering a self-guided tour.

Lake Lure offers a similar experience with its annual Dirty Dancing Festival. It includes shag and lake lift competitions.

Patrick Swayze (he passed away in 2009) had a great career, going on to star in such memorable films as *Roadhouse* (1989); *Ghost* (1990); *Point Break* (1991); *To Wong Foo, Thanks for Everything! Julie Newmar* (1995); and *Donnie Darko* (2001).

Jennifer Grey had a great supporting role in *Ferris Bueller's Day Off* (1986), but her films following *Dirty Dancing* were mostly forgettable. She did turn up recently in Jesse Eisenberg's Oscar-nominated *A Real Pain* (2024). And she showed up on TV's *Dancing with the Stars* (Baby didn't win).

"I love to dance," she says, "but I'm not great at it...."

She blamed her career fizzle on her nose job. Her schnozzle was a distinctive feature that she believed was a barrier to certain roles, particularly roles that weren't Jewish. She referred to it as her "pesky friend." After filming *Dirty Dancing*, Grey underwent a rhinoplasty.

And later, while filming *Wind* (1992), she noticed a small bump on her nose and underwent a second procedure to fix it, but the surgeon went further than she expected. Although a perfectly fine nose, she no longer looked like Jennifer Grey. She looked like any other Hollywood actress. "Overnight I lost my identity and my career," Grey bemoaned in her memoir, *Out of the Corner*.

She played herself in a short-lived television comedy (*It's Like, You Know...*) that was promoted as the California version of *Seinfeld*. The sitcom had a running gag that she didn't look like Jennifer Grey.

However, most agree the primary reason her career failed to take off was because she got into a huge car accident right before *Dirty Dancing* came out. On August 5, 1987, Grey and Matthew Broderick, who were dating at the time, were in a car crash in Ireland that killed two people. The trauma and PTSD caused her to lose focus on her Hollywood career. She took a hiatus from acting. By the time she got back into the swing, the heat from *Dirty Dancing* had dissipated.

"When I read the script there was so much that felt like it was made for me," says Grey. "There are so many layers to this movie. There is so much goodness under what feels like a fluffy rom-com fairytale. There is so much depth in the structure of the characters, and the relevance to what's going on right now."

Ironically, the studio hated the film. After viewing the rough cut, one of the producers suggested, "Burn the negative, and collect the insurance."

How wrong could a Hollywood exec be? A 2007 survey declared *Dirty Dancing* the number one Women's Most-Watched Film.

And, in 2024, the film was selected for preservation in the United States National Film Registry as being "culturally, historically, or aesthetically significant."

There are rumors about a possible *Dirty Dancing* sequel. Jennifer Grey plans to be part of it. When *Entertainment Weekly* asked her if the sequel would again be shooting at the Mountain Lake Lodge in Virginia, she replied, "I can't tell you that, but I can tell you that the movie will involve Kellerman's, so I would guess some of that is yes."

Knowing that a geological anomaly has caused Mountain Lake to shrink to barely more than a dry bed, let's hope the film's production returns to Lake Lure. After all, this lake still offers 720 acres of water as a background.

A little muddy these days. But Baby doesn't have to fall off a log this time around.

CHAPTER 2
It

Freightmeiser Stephen King lives in a spooky old house in Bangor, Maine. So, it's not surprising that many of his novels and short stories are set in that state.

It Chapter One (2017) and *It Chapter Two* (2019) are supernatural horror films based on Stephen King's *It*, a novel about a malicious clown named Pennywise. The story takes place in the fictional town of Derry, Maine.

The Losers Club – Bill, Ben, Richie, Eddie, Stan, Mike, and Bev – set out to investigate the disappearance of Bill's younger brother Georgie, only to come face to face with a shape-shifting monster that poses as a clown.

In these two latest adaptations, Bill Skarsgård plays Pennywise the Dancing Clown (A/K/A It). He says, "It's such an extreme character. Inhumane, It's beyond even a sociopath, because he's not even human. He's not even a clown. I'm playing just one of the beings It creates."

Derry, Maine, is the setting for a number of King's stories. He has said that Derry is actually his portrayal of Bangor.

The town of Derry was first mentioned in a 1981 short story "The Bird and the Album," but it was not until his 1986 novel *It* that the town appeared as "a fully rendered setting."

Besides the oft-used locations of Derry, Castle Rock, and Jerusalem's Lot, King has created other fictional Maine towns, including Haven, Little Tall Island, and Chester's Mill.

The motion picture version of *It* split the novel into two parts – *It Chapter One* and *It Chapter Two*.

Needing a small town in which to film the story, the producers picked Port Hope, Ontario, for most of the exterior shots. With over 270 heritage-designated buildings, Port Hope has a higher per capita rate of preservation than any other town or city in Canada.

For the movie, Port Hope's Walton Street and Queen Street substituted as Downtown Derry. The scene could be a small town in Maine, for all the moviegoer knows.

The Derry Cinema scenes were shot at the Capitol Theater at 20 Queens Street. Having undergone a $3-million renovation, the theater's main auditorium is decorated as a courtyard with clouds projected onto the ceiling.

The Nooks at 68 Walton Street was used for the pharmacy store. Quality Meats, where Mike makes a delivery, was also filmed on Walton Street. And Beverley's home is Queenies Bake Shop at 16 Walton Street.

The park where the kids gather is Memorial Park on Queens Street.

Derry Public Library, where Ben researches the town's history, was in fact the Port Hope Town Hall on Queens Street.

And the overgrown field beneath the railroad track is found in John Street.

With a population of just over 17,000, Port Hope is not a big town. All these locations are easy to find.

But some of the movie's scenes were shot elsewhere.

The synagogue was actually the Congregation Knesseth Israel in Toronto.

The Derry High school exteriors were filmed at the Mount Mary Retreat Centre in Ancaster, Ontario.

Other locations include the Scottish Rite Club in Hamilton, Ontario, and Audley Park in Ajax, Ontario.

The Barrens were filmed at Rouge Park in Scarborough, Toronto. The Barrens are a small tract of land still heavily covered in trees and plant life.

And exteriors for the so-called horror house were built on the same property in Oshawa, Ontario.

~ ~ ~

Despite its scenic qualities, Port Hope is known for having the largest volume of radioactive wastes in Canada. This was created by Eldorado Mining and Refining Limited, a result of refining radium from pitchblende.

During World War II, the Eldorado plant produced uranium oxides which were used in the Manhattan Project to make nuclear weapons. This plant continues to produce uranium fuel for nuclear power plants.

A proper site for a Stephen King horror story.

CHAPTER 3
The Ice Storm

Directed by Ang Lee, *The Ice Storm* (1997) is a family drama based on the same-named book by Rick Moody. A true story that took place during Thanksgiving 1973 in New Canaan, Connecticut, the movie follows two "dysfunctional upper-class families seeking escapism through alcohol, adultery, and sexual experimentation."

The plot: Ben Hood is dissatisfied with his marriage and his career. He's having an affair with his neighbor Janey Carver. Both families attend a "key party," where wives are swapped. Tensions rise as the mix-'em-match-'em takes unexpected turns. In the background, a winter ice storm descends over the community like a blanket.

The ensemble cast included Kevin Kline and Joan Allen as the Hoods; Jamey Sullivan and Sigourney Weaver as the Carvers. Tobey Maguire and Christina Ricci are the Hoods' children; Elijah Wood and Adam Hann-Byrd are cast as the Carvers' offspring.

Watching the movie, the question lingers: How does a gay Taiwanese director know so much about North American family life in the 1970s?

Ang Lee (*Eat Drink Man Woman*, *Sense and Sensibility*, *Brokeback Mountain*) puts it like this: "When you make a movie, you try to pretend. Think of it as actors. Kevin and Sigourney, I believe they never swapped wives before, yet they do their job in the movie. Actors playing different parts. The same thing goes for directors. I don't want to do the same movie over and over again – same thing, same story."

Apparently, he got everything right. *The Ice Storm* was nominated for several awards, notably winning the Palme d'or for Best Screenplay; a BAFTA and SFFCC for Sigourney Weaver as Best Supporting Actress; and the SIYAD, Gulbagge, and Bodil Awards for Best Film. And its theme song – "The Morning After" sung by Maureen McGovern – won an Oscar for Best Song.

Roger Ebert called *The Ice Storm* Ang Lee's best film yet, and Gene Siskel declared it his favorite film of 1997.

Principal photography for *The Ice Storm* took place in New Canaan, Connecticut, and nearby Westchester, New York. The houses belonging to Ben and Elena Hood and Jim and Janey Carver were filmed *in situ*. You can drive by them at your leisure.

Scenes involving the Hood's daughter riding her bike were filmed on Main Street (Elm Street) in New Canaan.

Varnum's Pharmacy and the New Canaan Library were also used for scenes in the film.

~ ~ ~

Segments at the Metro-North Railroad station (Ben taking the train to work and Paul being picked up) were shot at the picturesque station in New Canaan.

As it happened, I stood a few feet behind the cameras that day watching Kevin Kline do the train station scene. Being filmed in the heat of the summer, the train station was tricked out with fake snow on the roof and artificial icicles glued along the roofline. Kline was sweating in a heavy winter coat.

I kept one of the icicles as a souvenir. Still have it.

The real ice storm scenes in the movie were shot by a second-unit camera team, capturing footage of a blizzard that had hit the area the previous winter.

At the time, I lived on the state line, technically in South Salem, only a few miles from downtown New Canaan.

Located about an hour from New York City by train, the town of New Canaan is bounded on the south by Darien, to the west by Stamford, on the east by Wilton, on the southeast by Norwalk, and on the north by Westchester County, New York.

New Canaan is known for its architecture (it was an important center of the modern design movement from the late 1940s through the 1960s). The film shows off many of the town's modern houses, particularly a mostly glass house situated on Laurel Road. You'll recognize it in the movie.

Back then, the medium family income in New Canaan was $175,331 – one of the highest per capita households in the US. Of the 19,395 residents, 95.27% were White. Blonde, blue-eyed shoppers prowl the quaint streets, lunching in such eateries as Gates (black bean soup was David Letterman's favorite), Cherry Street East (it claimed to be haunted), Starbucks (I used to spot Susan Sarandon and Tim Robbins sipping Grandes there), and Solé (it prided itself at being as noisy as a New York restaurant; Bob Costas sometimes dined there).

Every Christmas Eve, residents sing carols on God's Acre, a town tradition since 1916. The famous slope lies at the foot of the Congregational Church on Park Street. We used to join them. Today, I have a lovely lithograph of the God's Acre carolers hanging in one of my guest bedrooms.

Lewis Lapham, a founder of Texaco – and the great-grandfather of long-time *Harper's Magazine* editor-in-chief Lewis H. Lapham – had an estate that is now New Canaan's 300-acre Waveny Park. At the time, I was Associate Publisher of *Harper's*, my office just down the hall from Lapham's.

William Randolph Hearst maintained a summer home for Marian Davis behind a hedge of bottle trees just off Highway 123. It had horse riding trails.

Nearby is Silver Hill, a private sanitorium that specializes in psychiatric and addictive disorders in tree-shaded seclusion. *Forbes* named Silver Hill one of the "Most Luxurious Places to Dry Out." Patients have included Jackie Kennedy's father, New York Yankees pitcher CC Sabathia, piano man Billy Joel, All-I-Want-for-Christmas singer Mariah Carey, and King of Pop Michael Jackson.

My wife met a shrink at the local nail saloon who assured her that all the dysfunction portrayed in *The Ice Storm* was accurate. Key clubs were common, she said. Should we feel insulted that we were never invited, I wondered?

~ ~ ~

New Canaan is easy to find, just off US 95 or the Merrick Parkway. The railway station where I watched Kevin Kline do his scene is found in the center of town.

But don't expect to feel welcomed.

One 4th of July, my wife and I were sitting on the hot sidewalk on New Canaan's Elm Street, waiting for the parade to start. A man came around, asking us to sign a political petition. When I explained that we technically lived on the other side of the state line, in New York, he frowned and said bluntly, "Don't they have places for you to shop over there?"

CHAPTER 4

A Christmas Story

A radio commentator named Jean Shepherd wrote some nostalgic stories about his midwestern childhood, which were collected into a book call *In God We Trust: All Others Pay Cash*. One of the stories became the basis of Bob Clark's 1983 movie, *A Christmas Story*.

Starring Peter Billingsley as Ralphie, a kid who wants Santa to bring him a Red Ryder air rifle, the film has become a Christmas classic.

"You'll shoot your eye out, kid" ranks #33 on Good Housekeeping's list of famous Christmas Movie Quotes.

"It was a small movie that really nobody wanted to make, and took filmmakers close to 12 years to get made," remembers Peter Billingsley. "I think it was just an afterthought for the studio at the time. Bob Clark, the director, had agreed to do other work for them to get it made, threw his whole salary in. It was really a labor of love. So, it's been very cool to see where it's come to — somewhat similar to *It's a Wonderful Life*."

Jean Shepherd co-wrote the script for *A Christmas Story* with his wife Leigh Brown and director Bob Clark. He also narrated the story in the guise of an adult version of Ralphie.

Although presented as a series of childhood vignettes, the main plot is about the air rifle. On Christmas morning, Ralphie Parker is disappointed not to find the air rifle under the tree. However, Ralphie's father ("The Old Man") points to one last box hidden in the corner, which contains the rifle. Ralphie tells us this was best Christmas present he had ever received or ever would receive.

The film is set in Hohman, Indiana, a fictionalized version of Shepherd's hometown of Hammond. In commemoration, the City of Hammond holds an annual festival in November and December. Hammond also exhibits a statue depicting the scene where Ralphie's friend Flick freezes his tongue to a flagpole.

However, the movie's exterior scenes were shot in Cleveland, Ohio. Bob Clark (*Porky's*, *Murder by Decree*) reportedly scouted 20 cities before selecting Cleveland, largely because Higbee's Department Store agreed to let him to film the infamous Santa Claus scene inside it.

Alas, you cannot visit this location. Higbee's became a Dillard's in 1992 and closed permanently in 2002.

But good news, you can visit Ralphie Parker's home. Located in the Tremont section of Cleveland's West Side, the house has been restored, reconfigured inside to match the soundstage interiors, and opened to the public as "A Christmas Story House."

The address for your car's GPS is 3159 West 11th Street in Cleveland.

In 2004, the 19th-century Victorian house was purchased on eBay for $150,000 by private developer Brian Jones and turned into a museum. Open year round, it is now a complex of five buildings devoted to the film.

Designed to be an interactive experience, you can recreate your favorite scenes from the movie: You're invited to "pose with the iconic leg lamp and replica BB gun, hide under the kitchen sink like Randy, or decode a secret message in the bathroom while washing your mouth out with Lifebuoy soap!"

The museum contains many props from the film, including the Parker family car, brother Randy's snow suit, the Higbee's window toys, the chalk board from Miss Shields' classroom, hundreds of behind-the-scenes photos, and one of only six custom-built Daisy Red Ryder BB guns used in the film. In addition, a 3,500-square-foot gift shop offers movie memorabilia and souvenirs.

Yes, you can buy a leg lamp.

I have one.

Turns out, Brian Jones owns the Red Rider Leg Lamp Company, which manufactures replicas of the "major award" Ralphie's father won in the film. Jones used revenues from his leg lamp business for the down payment on "A Christmas Story House."

The interior scenes in the movie were mostly filmed on a sound stage in Toronto. But Jones watched the movie frame by frame, drew up detailed plans, and spent an additional $240,000 to transform the rooms in "A Christmas Story House" into a near-replica of the movie set.

Due to licensing issues, the official name of the attraction was changed to "House from A Christmas Story" in 2023. I don't see much difference, but lawyers can split hairs.

In November 2023, Joshua Dickerson, a 16-year employee of the museum, became the museum's new owner. Continuing the tradition.

No need to look for a nearby hotel. You can stay at the "House from A Christmas Story" or next door at the "Bumpus House" if you choose. The Bumpus House offers two distinct accommodations: the "Hound Dog Haven" suite on the first floor (sleeps up to four guests) or the "Stolen Turkey" suite, spanning the second and third floors (sleeps up to six guests).

Located at 3159 W. 11th Street, the house was featured as the Bumpus family home in a sequel movie, *My Summer Story* (1994).

The franchise claims two other films – *A Christmas Story 2* (2012) and *A Christmas Story Christmas* (2022).

In case you want to visit these sets, *A Christmas Story 2* was filmed in New Westminster, British Columbia, Canada. The meat market scene was shot in the Gastown section of Vancouver. The department store scene was in the Vancouver train station.

And *A Christmas Story Christmas* (which features Peter Billingsley as a grown-up Ralphie) was filmed in Hungary and Bulgaria. To maintain the film's authenticity, the production team commissioned building an exact replica of the Parker House as well as the entire neighborhood block.

"We created 11 structures back there, including the Bumpus house," Billingsley says. "We built them from the ground up and really replicated old Cleveland Street."

Good luck finding them today. Word is, the Hungary and Bulgaria sets were destroyed after filming was completed.

In all, Jean Shepherd's stories about Ralphie Parker add up to a stage play, two theatrical films, four made-for-TV films, one straight-to-video film, one made-for streaming-video film, one live television musical, and one unaired TV pilot.

That's a lot of storytelling about a kid in search of a Red Ryder air rifle.

CHAPTER 5
Cape Fear

I grew up in North Carolina, so I'm familiar with Cape Fear, a tidewater area near Wilmington. A large portion of the region is low-lying wetlands such as the Green Swamp, one of the rare habitats for the Venus Flytrap. Matter of fact, I own a pet Venus Flytrap that I call Audrey.

The name Cape Fear comes from the 1585 expedition of Sir Richard Grenville, whose ship became embayed behind the cape. The crew were afraid they would wreck, giving rise to the expressive name. It is the fifth-oldest surviving English place name in the US.

In 1962, director J. Lee Thompson (*The Guns of Navarone*, *Battle for the Planet of the Apes*, *King Solomon's Mines*) made a psychological horror thriller titled *Cape Fear*. Based on a John D. McDonald novel called *The Executioners*, the film tells an edge-of-your-seat story about an ex-con named Max Cady who seeks revenge on attorney Sam Bowden by stalking his family. It's pretty scary.

The casting is perfect: straight-arrow Gregory Peck as the lawyer, Polly Bergen as his vulnerable wife, and Robert Mitchum as the over-the-top psychopath.

North Carolina's Cape Fear River wasn't a component of MacDonald's novel but was the invention of the film's director. "It adds desperation and tension to the ... film's final act," says Crooked Marquee's Roxana Hadadi. "Good versus evil, you might say. A comfortingly righteous Gregory Peck and an especially creepy Robert Mitchum are wonderfully oppositional throughout, and their physicality emboldens the concluding life-and-death duel."

However, the movie was not filmed in Cape Fear, North Carolina. The outdoor scenes mostly took place in Savannah, Georgia, and on the studio backlot at Universal City, California.

As it happens, tough-guy Mitchum had an aversion to filming in Savannah because as a teenager he had been arrested there for vagrancy and put on a chain gang. As a compromise, many of the outdoor scenes (and the fight on the houseboat at the end of the movie) were shot at Ladd's Marina in Stockton, California. A boat repair yard on the San Joaquin River, Ladd's offers easy access to the

California Delta, a vast network of waterways that stretch over 1,000 miles. It's very picturesque if you're a boater.

You'll find Ladd's Marina at 4911 Buckley Cove Way in Stockton.

~ ~ ~

Wait, there's more.

In 1991, Steven Spielberg had been scheduled to direct a remake of *Cape Fear*, but he decided it was much too violent for his taste (the harrowing Omaha Beach scene in *Saving Private Ryan* would come later), so he traded it off to Martin Scorsese in exchange for *Schindler's List*. A good swap, in that *Schindler's List* was nominated for twelve awards and won seven (including Best Picture, Best Director, and Best Adapted Screenplay). And Scorsese (*Taxi Driver*, *Raging Bull*, *Goodfellas*, *Casino*) was not squeamish about violence.

Oddly, Spielberg had wanted Bill Murray to play Max Cady, but Scorsese called on his go-to guy, Robert De Niro. Scorsese wanted Harrison Ford to play the lawyer, but Ford was only interested in doing the juicy psycho role. So, the part went to Nick Nolte.

Unlike the original film, where Gregory Peck reprised his Atticus Finch persona, Nolte's lawyer is a deeply flawed man who bears much of the responsibility for bringing Max Cady into his family's life. Jessica Lange was cast as the threatened wife; Juliette Lewis was perfect as the jailbait daughter.

Nolte lost weight for the role; De Niro gained muscle, so he would be properly intimidating when he faced off against Nolte who was taller. At the age of 48, De Niro went on a high-carb diet of brown rice and green vegetables to fuel marathon workout sessions that consisted of chin-ups, push-ups, and 600 crunches a day.

As an homage to the earlier film, Gregory Peck, Robert Mitchum, and Martin Balsam made cameo appearances. And Bernard Hermann's original score was re-orchestrated by Elmer Bernstein.

This was Gregory Peck's last movie role. It was also the seventh collaboration between Scorsese and De Niro. To date, the buds have done ten movies together.

Cape Fear was a commercial success and became the first Scorsese film to gross over $100 million. It got two Oscar nods (Best Actor for De Niro; Best Supporting Actress for Lewis) but won none.

Under Scorsese's direction, *Cape Fear* conveys a rapidly increasing sense of dread. Towards the end of the film, he relies on almost only closeups to increase the viewer's anxiety.

"He's using very dramatic camera moves, deliberately making them more visible to the eye," says Thelma Schoonmaker, Scorsese's long-time editor.

Both versions of *Cape Fear* were greatly influenced by Alfred Hitchcock's films – right down to the unusual camera angles, rapid zooms, lighting, and editing techniques. Also, the opening credits were designed by Saul Bass, who was a frequent Hitchcock collaborator. "Marty was going for that Gothic thriller look," says Schoonmaker.

A former altar boy who studied for the priesthood, Martin Scorsese has never been coy about his religious beliefs. He likes to delve into the questions of "what we believe, how we believe, and why we believe."

Scorsese uses Max Cady to explore this subtext in *Cape Fear*. Cady's devotion to a higher power is symbolized by his tattoos: a large cross, Bible verses, and words like "truth" and "justice." Scorsese worked closely with De Niro and artist Ilona Herman to identify Bible verses and designs for Cady's extensive body art.

Screenwriter Wesley Strict recalls that "Every scene of Bob's, he would call me up and say, 'Can Max say something else here about vengeance, from the Bible?'"

"I am like God, and God like me," proclaims Robert De Niro's Max Cady. He wields Bible verses "like weapons," notes Io Montecillo of Cultural Compass.

Cady is undeniably a bad man. But so is Sam Bowden, the lawyer who swore to defend Cady in court, but by withholding evidence landed him in prison for 14 years. Not surprising that the ex-convict wants revenge.

Roger Ebert concluded: "*Cape Fear* is impressive moviemaking, showing Scorsese as a master of a traditional Hollywood genre who is able to mold it to his own themes and obsessions."

Another critic observed, "The dissonance between the cultural expectations we associate with the Bible and our immediate perception of this character as evil contributes to the sustained horror of the film."

~ ~ ~

So, did Martin Scorsese return to the namesake location on the North Carolina coast to film this remake? No, he filmed this version of *Cape Fear* in Florida, mostly around Fort Lauderdale and its suburb of Dania. You'll recognize some of the street scenes if you drive around the town.

Other locations included I-95 north of Miami, and in the Everglades. If you want to visit, the main entrance to the Everglades National Park is on Route SR 9336 from Florida City, or off Route 41 at Shark Valley and Everglades City.

You can easily find New Essex High School, where Cady seduces Bowden's 14-year-old daughter into "a bout of finger-sucking." It's really Broward College. You'll come across the school just east of the Rolling Hills Golf Club (where the Chevy Chase comedy *Caddyshack* was filmed).

The ice cream store where Cady threateningly shows up is really the Rainbo Café, found at 1909 Hollywood Boulevard in West Broward. It's a good place for breakfast.

And the scene where Cady clings to the underside of the family car was filmed at the Seminole Indian Truck Stop at 4690 Orange Drive (North US Highway 27) near SW 45th Street in Weston. A convenience store and gas station, as well as a Subway franchise and a thatched-hut tiki bar with live music, it remains a favorite pit stop for long-haul truckers.

Recently, I made a road trip to visit a colleague in Wilmington, North Carolina, diverting myself to spend a few hours on Cape Fear. There in the swampy underbrush, where the Venus Flytraps grow, it seemed quite spooky. Not a place I'd want to run into a guy like Max Cady.

CHAPTER 6
X-Men

Years back, I was handpicked by Stan Lee to succeed him as Publisher of Marvel Comics. The largest comic book company in the world, we published the amazing adventures of Spider-Man, Iron Man, the Avengers, Hulk, the X-Men, and other superheroes.

Being a fanboy, I knew that in the comic books Professor X maintained a School for Gifted Youngsters (read: mutants) in Salem Center, located in Westchester County, New York. Stan always placed his characters in real-life settings like New York City ... or Salem, New York.

At the time I lived in South Salem, so I pretended the X-Men were hanging out only a few houses down the street.

The address for Professor X's school was 1407 Graymalkin Lane. I never did find it.

As you know, Marvel Studios brought these superheroes to the silver screen with the Marvel

Cinematic Universe (MCU). That was the umbrella concept that turned the characters into a repertoire company. The studio folks appropriated that device from the comic books.

We used to say if you saw thunderclouds in one comic book, it would be raining in the next comic book. All the stories took place in one universe, the characters interacting.

Salem Center aside, if you really want to visit the setting for Charles Xavier's School for Gifted Youngsters, you'll have to go to Canada. Hatley Castle in British Columbia has been used for exterior shots of the school in numerous *X-Men* films.

Easy to find, Hatley Park National Historic Site is located in Colwood, British Columbia, in Greater Victoria.

Hatley Castle is a Scottish baronial-style mansion that was built in 1908 by James Dunsmuir, the province's former premier. The castle was purchased by the government in 1940, with plans to relocate King George VI and his family here during the World War II, but the UK decided that it would be too demoralizing for the Royal Family to leave England at that time.

The castle has a history as a military college and as a university, which you can learn more about by taking a guided walking tour of the grounds.

From the 1940s to 1995, it served as a naval training facility. But after the Cold War, the facility was decommissioned.

In 1995, the Royal Roads University Act was passed, establishing Royal Roads University, a small public college that offers over 70 programs, ranging from certificates and diplomas to undergraduate and graduate degrees. RRU currently has an enrollment of about 4,100 students.

The castle also houses a small Canadian military museum.

Hatley Castle has been featured as the Xavier Institute in both the 1996 television film *Generation X*, and in the X-Men film franchise – including *X2: X-Men United*; *X-Men: The Last Stand*; *Deadpool*; and *Deadpool 2*.

While you're in the area, you may want to visit some other *X-Men* filming sites.

For example, the University of British Columbia at 800 Robson Street in Vancouver, British Columbia, was used in *X2: X-Men United* for a scene where blue-skinned shapeshifting Mystique breaks into a government building.

And the Stave Falls Powerhouse in Mission was used as the engine room at Alkali Lake in *X2: X-Men United*.

Want more? Golden Ears Provincial Park in British Columbia, was the forest where Magneto encamped in *X-Men: The Last Stand*. And the house at 1769 Golf Club Drive, Tsawwassen, Delta, British Columbia became Jean Grey's childhood home in *X-Men: The Last Stand*.

Many of the interior shots for Xavier's School for Gifted Youngsters took place inside Casa Loma, a Gothic Revival castle and garden found at 1 Austin Place in Toronto. Now a historic museum, it was constructed in the early 1900s as a residence for financier Sir Henry Pellatt. The unique mansion is popular for filming movies and television programs.

More?

If you're willing to travel afar, you can find several X-Men locations in New Zealand.

Dunedin in Otago was the location of Cassidy's Bar in *X-Men Origins: Wolverine*. And a shack at Deer Park Heights in Queenstown, Otago, served as Wolverine's cabin in the Canadian Rockies in *X-Men Origins: Wolverine*.

Australia claims some locations, too.

A forest in Camden, New South Wales, Australia, substituted as the Angola jungle in *X-Men Origins: Wolverine*. And Federal Park, Glebe, in Sydney, Australia, provide the locale for the carnival scenes in *X-Men Origins: Wolverine*.

Tired of chasing the X-Men around the globe? Then just visit the Golden Gate Bridge in San

Francisco. That provided background shots for *X-Men: The Last Stand.*

As for me, I'm still poking around South Salem for any signs of Wolverine or Professor Charles Xavier.

CHAPTER 7
Fargo

The movie was going to be called *Brainerd*. After all, much of it was filmed around Brainerd, Minnesota. But then Joel and Ethan Cohen (*O Brother Where Art Thou*, *No Country for Old Men*, *Raising Arizona*) had the epiphany that *Brainerd* was not a cool name for a movie. So, instead, they called it *Fargo*.

Fargo is 138 miles from Brainerd.

The Cohen Brothers (sometimes referred to as "the director with two heads") are from Minnesota, born and raised in St. Louis Park, a suburb of Minneapolis.

"Minnesota is known for having a whole bunch of mosquitos, a giant list of lakes, and of course Mayo Clinic," muses Carly Ross, a DJ at Rochester's 106.9 KROC. "But it would have been pretty sweet to have a movie named after a Minnesota town!"

Fargo, as you may know, is the largest city in North Dakota, located in the southeastern part of the state, across the Red River, just north of Moorhead, Minnesota. Fargo has a population of more than 125,000. The average annual temperature is 43.3°F. The average high in January is 19°F. Fargo receives an average of 40 inches of snow per year.

However, very little of the movie *Fargo* takes place in Fargo.

Fargo (1996) is a black comedy crime film. In it, a Minneapolis car dealer named Jerry Lundegaard (William H. Macy) hires two thugs (Steve Buscemi and Peter Stormare) to kidnap his wife, expecting to collect a fat ransom from her wealthy father (Harve Presnell).

Being that this is a Coen Brothers film, it's easy to guess that the criminals are not very bright and that things quickly spiral out of control. Their plans go awry when a pregnant Minnesota police chief named Marge Gunderson (Frances McDormand, wife of Joel Coen) begins investigating a series of roadside homicides that ensue from their botched crimes.

And, yes, it involves a woodchipper.

"*Fargo* is a movie about deceit, about how people lie to each other for personal gain," says Jacob Park of Fan Theories. "The Cohen Brothers do that too. The opening frames of *Fargo* announce that the movie is based on a true story ... but it isn't."

"This is a true story. The events depicted in this film took place in Minnesota in 1987. At the request of the survivors, the names have been changed. Out of respect for the dead, the rest has been told exactly as it occurred."

Liar, liar, pants on fire.

"Marketing this film as a true story makes it more compelling and shocking," says Park. "The Coen Brothers are trying to show that anybody can trick and deceive you, even your favorite movie directors."

"We wanted to make a movie just in the genre of a true story movie," explained Ethan Coen. "You don't have to have a true story to make a true story movie." In short, the brothers wanted the film to convey the feeling of being a sordid true-crime drama even if it wasn't.

If you look closely, you'll find a handful of other lies and deliberately incorrect facts scattered throughout the tricky film.

My favorite is the statement that "the Bark Beetle carries a worm to its nest, where it will feed its young for up to six months." As it happens, Bark Beetles do not eat worms. Like their name implies, they eat bark.

After graduating from Bard's College in Great Barrington, Massachusetts, the Coen Brothers went separate ways. Joel spent four years in the undergraduate film program at New York University, where he made a 30-minute thesis film, *Soundings*. Ethan went on to Princeton University where he earned an undergraduate degree in philosophy, his 48-page senior thesis titled "Two Views of Wittgenstein's Later Philosophy."

After NYU, Joel worked as a production assistant on a variety of industrial films and music videos. Then the brothers teamed up to make an indie crime drama called *Blood Simple* (1984). It won the Sundance Film Festival Grand Jury Prize. And the Cohen Brothers won the Independent Spirit Award for Best Director.

The Coen Brothers are known for jumping from genre to genre. As film critic Richard Corless described them: "Dexterously flipping and reheating old movie genres like so many pancakes, they serve them up fresh, not with syrup but with a coating of comic arsenic."

Fargo was filmed during the winter of 1995. Due to unusually low snowfall in central and southern Minnesota that winter, scenes requiring snow-covered landscapes had to be shot in northern Minnesota and northeastern North Dakota.

When I went looking for *Fargo* movie locations, I was dismay with how many are gone.

For example, the King of Clubs – the pool bar where the financially desperate car salesman meets up with the two miscreants to arrange the kidnapping of his wife – has been demolished and replaced by housing. You can drive by where it stood at 957 Central Avenue NE at 3rd Avenue NE, in northeast Minneapolis.

Also gone is Gustafson Motors where Jerry worked as salesman. The real car lot of Wally McCarthy Oldsmobile is now the campus of Best Buy. You can visit its former location at the northeast junction of I-494 at Penn Avenue in Richfield, a southern suburb of Minneapolis.

The giant statue of Paul Bunyan was built just for the film – and was dismantled after filming. It stood near the Canadian border on Pembina County Highway 1, four miles west of Bathgate, North Dakota.

The "Blue Ox Truckstop," where the two kidnappers meet up with a couple of hookers, was filmed at Stockmen's Truck Stop, located at 501 Farwell Avenue in South St. Paul. Still there, it's a great place to grab a quick meal.

However, Ember's Restaurant, which stood at 7527 Wayzata Boulevard at Pennsylvania Avenue South in the St Louis Park area of Minneapolis, is no longer there. This is where Jerry sits down with his father-in-law to discuss the ransom for his wife.

The cabin on Square Lake in May, Minnesota, where Jerry's wife was being held captive, has been relocated. I never found out where.

The Brainerd Police Station was the old Edina Police Station. Located at 4801 West 50th Street, in Edina, it has been completely rebuilt. You won't recognize it.

Nonetheless, there are still a few landmarks you can visit.

The scene at the Carlton Celebrity Room, where José Feliciano was performing, was staged at the Chanhassen Dinner Theater at 501 West 78th Street in Chanhassen. Located about 25 minutes southwest of downtown Minneapolis, you'll find the theatre two blocks north of Minnesota State Highway 5 on Great Plains Boulevard.

The ransom drop site on top the roof of the "Radisson Hotel" was in fact atop the parking structure on 3rd Avenue South at South 8th Street, in downtown Minneapolis.

The house of Mr. Mohra can be found on 3rd Street South at the corner of Bryan Avenue, in the shadow of the giant grain elevator on Highway 75 in Hallock.

The Lakeside Club, where Officer Gunderson questions the hookers, is still standing on Old Wildwood Road, outside of Mahtomedi.

The Hitching Post Motel was the stand-in for "the motel outside Bismarck" where Jerry is apprehended. You can still find it at 23855 Forest Boulevard North in Forest Lake.

What about Fargo itself? Although there was no filming there, the Fargo-Moorhead Convention & Visitors Bureau at 2001 44th Street South in Fargo displays copies of the movie script and other memorabilia from the film – as well as the movie's actual woodchipper.

In 1998, the American Film Institute ranked *Fargo* among the 100 greatest American movies.

When pushed to identify the true crime that served as a basis for *Frago*, the Cohen Brothers point to the grizzly 1986 murder of Helle Crafts, a flight attendant from Connecticut, whose husband Richard disposed of her body with a wood chipper.

The spinoff TV series *Fargo* pays homage to the movie by displaying a similar "true story" disclaimer at the beginning of each episode. They lie, too. All the stories are fictional.

CHAPTER 6

Being There

It was maybe 14 the first time I visited Biltmore House, but I paid little attention to its Châteauesque architecture and Gilded Age opulence. My eyes were focused on a cute freckle-faced girl on the church tour bus. I had a pubescent crush on her. I got a kiss on the ride home.

When I returned to Biltmore over half a century later, as a journalist writing a travel article for *The Saturday Evening Post*, I gained an entirely new appreciation for this magnificent 255-room French Renaissance-style chateau with its steeply pitched roof, stately turrets, and sculptural ornamentation. Built by George W. Vanderbilt II between 1889 and 1895, it's situated on 8,000 acres of rolling mountain land adjacent to Asheville, North Carolina.

Billed as the largest privately owned home in the United States (it's still owned by Vanderbilt descendants, but none of them lives there), it boasts 178,926 square feet of floorspace.

Designed by noted architect Richard Morris Hunt, Biltmore House was patterned after Chateau de Blois, Chenonceau, and Chambord in France and Waddesdon Manor in England. The mansion cost $5 million to construct (equivalent to about $190 million today). Building the main house required about 1,000 workers and 60 stonemasons. Using Indiana limestone, a 375-foot-tall facade was designed to fit into the mountainous topography.

The grounds were landscaped by Frederick Law Olmsted, the same guy who landscaped New York's Central Park.

A 3-mile railroad spur was constructed to bring materials to the building site. A Tudor village was erected outside the estate's gates to house the workers. It morphed into a quaint collection of boutiques, galleries, and eateries until it was recently flooded by Hurricane Helene.

Vanderbilt made numerous trips overseas to purchase décor for his new summer home – tapestries, carpets, prints, linens, and rare *objets d'art*.

In 1930, Vanderbilt's daughter Cornelia and her husband agreed to open Biltmore to the public. This was at the request of the City of Asheville, which hoped to revitalize the area following the Great Depression with tourism.

The house contains the Vanderbilt's collection of paintings. These include works by Botticelli, Rembrandt, Gilbert Stuart, and Claude Monet.

~ ~ ~

Recently, I returned to Biltmore House. Standing there on the manicured hillside overlooking Biltmore House, the four-story, asymmetrically balanced facade with two projecting wings connecting to the entrance tower looked familiar. The stone decorations include trefoils, rosettes, gargoyles, and grotesques struck a chord of memory. Not a reminder of my previous visit, but instead a memory of a scene from a movie.

Being There (1979) was one of several motion pictures filmed at Biltmore Estates. Based on the 1971 novel by Jerzy Kosiński, it tells the story of Chance the Gardiner, a simpleton who is mistaken for a man of great wisdom. Coming to live at the palatial estate (Biltmore House) of his wealthy friend Ben, Chauncey Gardiner as he is now known becomes an advisor to the President of the United States. His naïve observations about gardening are interpreted as great insights into the world of politics.

The Academy Award-winning satire was directed by Hal Ashby (*In the Heat of the Night, Coming Home, Harold and Maude*). *Being There* gave Peter

Sellers "a well-received role after many felt he had lapsed into self-parody."

Melvyn Douglas won an Oscar for Best Supporting Actor for his portrayal of Ben. Peters Sellars was nominated for Best Actor for his role as Chauncey Gardiner.

According to co-star Shirley MacLaine, "Peter believed he was Chauncey. He never had lunch with me … He was Chauncey Gardiner the whole shoot, but believing he was having a love affair with me."

The Biltmore Estate served as the location for the wealthy industrialist's home in the film. You can easily find it on the south side of Asheville on Route 25, three blocks north from Highway 40. There's plenty of signage.

There was a scene at Asheville-Buncombe Technical College.

Filming also took place in Washington, DC. You can find the house at 937 M Street NW, which served as the exterior of Chance's earlier home.

And many interior scenes were shot at the Fenyes Mansion, located at 160-170 Orange Grove Boulevard in Pasadena, California. This is a route once known as "Millionaire's Row." The two-acre estate complex is not difficult to find – it's the headquarters of the Pasadena Historical Society.

Other interior shots took place at the Craven Estate at 430 Madeline Avenue in Pasadena. This building is also maintained by the Pasadena Museum of History.

The Biltmore House has appeared in several other movies. You can see it as the stand-in for the estate of Mason Verger (Gary Oldman) in Ridley Scott's *Hannibal* (2001). Others include *The Private Eyes* (1980), *Mr. Destiny* (1990), *The Last of the Mohicans* (1992), *Forrest Gump* (1994), *Richie Rich* (1994), *My Fellow Americans* (1996), *Patch Adams* (1998), and *The Odd Life of Timothy Green* (2012).

The Hallmark Channel has launched a series of movies set at Biltmore House, the first being *A Biltmore Christmas* (2023). Although other productions have been filmed at the property, these Hallmark productions mark the first time the National Historic Landmark has appeared in movies as the actual Biltmore Estates.

All that aside, most people will agree that the most famous movie ever filmed at Biltmore Estates was *The Swan* (1956), a romantic dramedy starring Grace Kelly. Directed by Charles Vidor, it was a remake of a 1925 silent film.

The story gives us a princess (Grace Kelly) who tries flirting with a doctor (Louis Jourdan) in order to trick a prince (Alex Guinness) into marrying her.

The movie provided a good rehearsal for Grace Kelly, who became a real-life princess when she married Prince Rainier Louis Henri Maxence

Bertrand Grimaldi of Monaco. MGM held up the release of *The Swan* to correspond with the civil wedding ceremony of Grace Kelly and Prince Rainier on April 18, 1956.

  Good marketing.

  Life imitating art.

CHAPTER 9

Breaking Away

Bloomington, Indiana, is a small college town. With about 45,000 students, Indiana University Bloomington is the flagship campus of the Indiana University system.

Bloomington was the location of the 1979 movie *Breaking Away*, featuring a reenactment of Indiana University's annual Little 500 bicycle race. Also known as the "Little Five," this is a track cycling race held during the third weekend of April at the Bill Armstrong Stadium. Modeled on the Indianapolis 500, riders compete in four-person teams around a quarter-mile cinder track.

The Little 500 was dramatized in *Breaking Away*, a story about a group of Bloomington townies who enter the race as the "Cutters" and defeat the favored fraternity teams.

The name comes from the local limestone cutters, Indiana townies who work cutting rock in the local limestone quarries. The movie's production team decided to call them "cutters" because they worried that the actual nickname ("stoners" or "stonies") would sound like a reference to drug usage to audiences not familiar with the area.

Following the release of *Breaking Away*, the cycling team of the college's Delta Chi fraternity "left their house amidst a fallout and took the name Cutters as their now 'independent' team moniker." They won their first race (in 1984). The new team is now made up of students who are either Bloomington locals or at the very least non-Greek. They have been very successful, winning fifteen races that they have entered. With an average finish of 3.7, the Cutters have never finished worse than 12th.

~ ~ ~

Directed by Peter Yates (*Bullitt*, *The Hot Rock*) and written by Steve Tesich (*Eyewitness*, *The World According to Garp*), *Breaking Away* starred Dennis Christopher, Dennis Quaid, Daniel Stern (in his film debut), Jackie Earle Haley, Paul Dooley, John Ashton, Robin Douglas, PJ Soles, and Barbara Barrie.

Tesich won an Academy Award for Best Original Screenplay, and the film was nominated for Best Picture. Barbara Barrie got a nod for Best Supporting Actress. Dennis Christopher won a BAFTA Award as Best Promising Newcomer.

Dirty Dancing In An Ice Storm

As an Indiana University graduate, Steve Tesich had served as an alternate rider for Phi Kappa Psi in the 1962 Little 500. His teammate Dave Blase rode 139 of 200 laps and was the victorious rider crossing the finish line. Blase became the model for the main character in *Breaking Away*.

Played by skinny, blond-haired Dennis Christopher, we see cyclist "Dave Stohler" as a romantic opera-singing teen. Like the character, Blase had an appreciation Italian culture and the Italian cycling team. The working title for the film had been *Bambino*.

Breaking Away has been described as "a *Rocky* for cyclist."

Although cycling professionally after leaving college, Blase eventually settled down as a high school biology teacher.

~ ~ ~

If you want to follow in the bicycle tracks of the movie's Dave Stohler, just make your way down to Bloomington. Located 40 miles southwest of Indianapolis, the city can be accessed from two major highways: Interstate 64, which runs north-south from Indianapolis to Interstate 64; and Indiana State Road 46, which runs east-west from Columbus to Terre Haute.

Once there, every filming location is within easy reach – either by car or by bicycle.

The house of wannabe-Italian Dave Stoller (Dennis Christopher) and his concerned parents can be found at 756 South Lincoln Street, southwest of downtown Bloomington.

A few blocks further southwest, "Campus Cars," his father's used car lot was created at 1010 South Walnut Street. No longer there, the car lot has been replaced by a couple of buildings.

In the film, the Cutters go looking for a fight with the college boys at the Student Union dining hall in the Indiana University Memorial Union Building, 900 East 7th Street, on the IU campus.

The Cutters run over the frisbee with their car at 101 North Jordan Avenue.

Dave runs a red light on his bike while going south on College Avenue just past the 5th Street intersection.

The Cinzano Bike Race Start Line was roughly at East 3rd Street and South Park Ridge Road.

The Little 500 Race was held at 1310 East 10th Street, but there's an Arboretum there now instead of a track. The building seen is the background is the Herman B. Wells Library.

The pizza restaurant where the guys hang out (now known as Opie Taylor's) is located on Bloomington's downtown square at 110 North Walnut Street.

Dave sees his dream girl drop a book as she gets on her moped in front of Franklin Hall, but today there's no longer a street in front of that campus building.

Siam House (formerly the Magic Horn), where Dave and Katherine (Robyn Douglas) grab a bite is located at 430 East 4th Street, just west of the campus.

To his friends' dismay, Dave serenaded his "Katarina" in Italian at the Delta Delta Delta sorority house, located at 818 East 3rd Street.

Rose Well House is the stone pavilion (built using the old gates of the university) where Dave gets up the nerve to reveal to Katherine that he's not Italian, but a Cutter. You can find it deep in Dunn's Woods, on the Old Crescent on the Indiana University campus.

Moocher (Jackie Earle Haley) and his girlfriend apply for a marriage license at the Monroe County Courthouse, 100 West Kirkwood Avenue, at North College Avenue.

Moocher's house was located at 170 East 7th Street, but it's no longer there. Gentrification.

Particularly iconic is cliff-sided Saunders Quarry, the water-filled limestone basin where Dave and his Cutter pals like to swim. They fiercely defend it when local students discover their favorite site. There are plenty of old limestone quarries in the area, but this one is found a few miles south of town, just off East Empire Mill Road.

The Saunders Quarry is private property. Please be careful if you go swimming in a quarry. Diving into quarries can be extremely dangerous, and there have been fatalities.

And I don't recommend drifting behind a semi-truck to get your bike up to 60 MPH. Stick to a race track like the one at the Bill Armstrong Stadium.

CHAPTER 10

A Place in the Sun

My wife's family was having a reunion in the middle of the Mojave Desert, a little oasis of a town known as Yucca Valley. Her folks had retired near there. Their house was too small to accommodate the families of nine children and assorted friends.

Rather than stay at the local Motel 6, Diane and I booked a room in Palm Springs, that fashionable resort some 27 miles southwest of Yucca Valley. The hotel was called A Place in the Sun, named after the 1951 film starring Elizabeth Taylor, Montgomery Cliff, and Shelly Winters.

"Welcome, dawlings," gushed the flamboyantly gay host in a startlingly pink sweater. "You're going to love it here, truly you will."

The courtyard-style motel is garishly colorful, framing a heated blue pool and punctuated by tall stately palm trees. The saltwater pool and jacuzzi area are quaint throwbacks to the 1950s. A Ponderosa lemon tree dominates one side of the grassy courtyard, and guests are encouraged to pick lemons and add them to their drinks.

The rooms were clean, but there were signs of age — a slightly flimsy quality. But that was to be expected for a structure that wasn't meant to be permanent in the first place. Built in the late '40s, it served as a resting spot for the cast and crew of the classic film, *A Place in the Sun*.

During the Golden Age of Hollywood, many actors' contracts included a "two-hour rule," a stipulation in old movie contracts that actors had to be within a two-hour drive of Los Angeles during production, which made Palm Springs a popular getaway for celebrities.

Palm Springs was convenient. Located in the heart of "Hollywood's Desert Playground" at 754 East San Lorenzo Road, the hotel is a lovingly preserved, mid-20th century historical set of 17 bungalows. This collection of extra-large rooms sprawls across a one-acre private palm tree park garden. Offering such amenities as a professional putting green, jacuzzi, and a poolside gazebo with an incredible view of the nearby mountains, you're only a stroll away from shopping, dining, theatres, and nightclubs.

Nearby is the Palm Springs Aerial Tramway; the Boomers Miniature Golf, Bumper Cars, and Arcades;

and the Wet N Wild Water Park. You can also book celebrity tours.

Or you can simply stay close to home base and hang out at the pool. Feel free to practice your putts on the hotel's artificial turf green. The front desk has golf clubs you can borrow.

~ ~ ~

Wedged between South Riverside Drive and East San Lorenzo Road, the "boutique resort" was easy to find. Parking was available on both sides.

Although adults only, A Place in the Sun is pet friendly. The manager's fluffy little designer dog yipped across the yard to greet us. The hotel's promotions encourage guests to "bring your dog and enjoy the green space, especially the grassy areas of some of the private patios." The hotel also sells doggie wear.

A collage of items from *A Place in the Sun* hangs in the hotel's lobby. It features movie promotions and an autograph from actress Anne Revere, who played Hannah Eastman in the film.

Front desk man Adrian Van Meeteren, whose parents Norma and Ron Van Meeteren own the property, smiles as he recounts that "Studios 14, 15, and 16 were built later on in between the existing units, but we have so many guests who ask for the same room numbers over the years, we've had to keep all the old room numbers, so when you look at the new studios, the numbers look out of sequence."

But, lounging by the pool, soaking up the sun, who's counting?

~ ~ ~

The movie was based on the 1925 novel *An American Tragedy* by Theodore Dreiser. There had been a 1926 play, and then a 1931 film, based on the novel, but it was the 1951 George Stevens film that offered the great star power – Elizabeth Taylor, Montgomery Cliff, and Shelly Winters.

Life Magazine said, "It gives three young actors the chance to give the most natural performances of their careers."

A Place in the Sun was inspired by the real-life 1906 trial of Chester Gillette, a man convicted of murdering his co-worker, Grace Brown. The two had been romantically involved, but when Brown became pregnant, Gillette left her for a wealthy socialite. That did not go well.

Similarly, the movie tells the story of George Eastman (Montgomery Cliff) who goes to work for his wealthy uncle. Despite a strict admonition not to date any of his co-workers., George becomes involved with both frumpy Alice Tripp (Shelley Winters) and glamorous Angela Vickers (Elizabeth Taylor). One of them dies. The question is: Did George commit murder?

Described as "a gripping tale of the power of greed, passion and perilous young love," *A Place in the Sun* won six Academy Awards: Best Director; Best Cinematography, Black &White; Best Costume Design, Black & White; Best Film Editing; Best Original Score; and Best Writing, Screenplay. It was also nominated for Best Picture, Best Actor for Montgomery Clift, and Best Actress for Shelley Winters.

Also, *A Place in the Sun* won the first-ever Golden Globes award for Best Motion Picture – Drama.

Turner Classic Movies calls *A Place in the Sun* "the quintessential drama, one of the best films of the era." Charlie Chaplin considered it "the greatest movie ever made about America."

In his book *Bambi vs. Godzilla: On the Nature, Purpose, and Practice of the Movie Business*, writer-director David Mamet included *A Place in the Sun* in a list of "four perfect films," alongside *The Godfather*, *Galaxy Quest*, and *Dodsworth*.

Elizabeth Taylor was only 17 years old when she starred in *A Place in the Sun*. Montgomery Cliff was 29. Liz became infatuated with Monty, but he was gay. Nonetheless, she formed a deep and lasting friendship with him. Director George Stevens played on their intense emotions, resulting in "powerful scenes of smoldering sexuality."

Shelley Winters changed her appearance for her role as Alice, shifting from her signature "blonde bombshell" look to that of a dowdy loser. As noted, her performance won her a nod for Best Actress, which she lost to Vivien Leigh for *A Streetcar Named Desire*. Winters would go on to win two Oscars, for *The Diary of Anne Frank* (1959) and *A Patch of Blue* (1965). She didn't take it too seriously. Less than six months later, she would be appearing in two episodes of the campy *Batman* television series.

~ ~ ~

A Place in the Sun was shot on a $2.3 million budget, mainly on Paramount's backlot at 5555 Melrose Avenue in Los Angeles. The film's location shooting took place at Lake Tahoe, along with some scenes at Echo Lake and Cascade Lake.

The exteriors of the Eastman factory were filmed at the Goodyear Tire factory at 6701 South Central Avenue at 69th Street in Los Angeles.

Although the film was made in 1949, it wasn't released until 1951 to avoid competing with Billy Wilder's *Sunset Boulevard*.

~ ~ ~

Although originally built as a production hideaway for the cast and crew, the hotel has become a beloved getaway for loyal guests who return year after year. I think I could be one of them.

CHAPTER 11
The Hunger Games

My brother-in-law Tony pulled his car off to the side of a dirt road and got out. "Here you are," he said. "The film set for *The Hunger Games*."

The scene looked desolate, a scattering of empty houses and storefronts on a sloping hillside that dipped down to the small gorge of the Henry River.

An abandoned village about 50 miles northwest of Charlotte, Henry River Mill Village served as "District 12" in *The Hunger Games*. Here, you will recognize the home of Katniss Everdeen (Jennifer Lawrence) as well as the Bakery where Peeta (Josh Hutcherson) toiled.

Built in the 1920s as a planned community with its own textile mill, dam, and company store, the buildings can be seen scattered along Henry River Road just to the south of Hildebran. The deserted homes were in a deteriorating state, the paint peeling, boards missing, roofs sagging.

A ghost town, the land it stands on is private. But sometimes tours are available. And you can arrange to spend the night at the restored Mill House. There are two units, each with a queen-sized bed, two twin beds, a kitchenette with microwave and refrigerator, and full-sized bathrooms.

The Henry River Mill Village Historic District is prime example of a typical textile mill town in the Carolinas. It was added to the National Register of Historic Places on May 9, 2019.

While the Henry River was used for waterpower as early as 1860, the land was developed in 1905 when the Aderholdt and Rudisill families partnered to establish the Henry River Manufacturing Company to produce cotton yarn During its initial operation, the company erected 35 worker houses, a two-story boarding house, a bridge, a brick company store, a power producing dam, and the original 3-story brick mill building where the yarn was manufactured.

Until 1914, the operations were driven by waterpower. Later, this was converted to steam power and electricity as upgrades were made to increase production. By the 1960s, the Company had begun a downward spiral due to economic pressures from overseas. The mill ceased operations shortly after that.

In 1977, just after Wade R. Sheppard purchased the property, the mill building burned down due to a lightning strike.

The last resident moved out by the early 2000s. The village was a collection of empty houses.

Then came the film crew.

~ ~ ~

The Hunger Games was adapted from Suzanne Collins' popular series of dystopian novels aimed at the Young Adult audience. The story takes place in a post-war nation known as Panem (which used to be the USA). It consists of a decadently wealthy Capitol and 12 poverty-stricken districts which are being punished for their part in the earlier uprising.

District 12, where the films' story begins, is supposedly a coal-mining region in the eastern US that stretches from Pennsylvania to Alabama – i.e., Appalachia. According to Suzanne Collins, Katniss Everdeen's home, District 12, was the poorest, smallest district in Panem. A perfect location to film the movie, Western North Carolina is a part of Appalachia.

The plot tells us that every year, the Capitol of Panem forces each of the 12 districts to send a boy and girl Tribute between the ages of 12 and 18 to compete in the Hunger Games – "a nationally televised event in which the Tributes fight each other to the death until one survivor remains."

When Primrose Everdeen is picked, her older sister Katniss volunteers to take her place. As a combatant in the Hunger Games, Katniss is forced to rely on her sharp instincts when pitted against highly trained Tributes from the other districts.

So far, there have been four films and a prequel – *The Hunger Games* (2012), *The Hunger Games: Catching Fire* (2013), *The Hunger Games: Mockingjay – Part 1* (2014), *The Hunger Games: Mockingjay – Part 2* (2015), and *The Hunger Games: The Ballad of Songbirds & Snakes* (2023).

Another prequel – *The Hunger Games: Sunrise on the Reaping* – is in the works, promised for 2026.

The original franchise features an ensemble cast that included Jennifer Lawrence as Katniss Everdeen, Josh Hutcherson as Peeta Mellark, Liam Hemsworth as Gale Hawthorne, Woody Harrelson as Haymitch Abernathy, Elizabeth Banks as Effie Trinket, Stanley Tucci as Caesar Flickerman, and Donal Sutherland as Panem's President Snow.

The prequel gives us Tom Blyth stars as Coriolanus Snow, Rachel Zegler as Lucy Gray Baird, Josh Andrés Rivera as Sejanus Plinth, Hunter Schafer as Tigris Snow, Peter Dinklage as Casca Highbottom, Viola Davis as Dr. Volumnia Gaul, and Jason Schwartzman as Lucretius "Lucky" Flickerman.

The first three films set box office records. *The Hunger Games* enjoyed the biggest opening day and biggest opening weekend for a non-sequel. *Catching Fire* set the record for biggest opening weekend of November. *Mockingjay – Part 1* had the largest opening day and weekend of 2014.

Mockingjay – Part 2 was praised for Jennifer Lawrence's performance. But the prequel – *The Ballad of Songbirds & Snakes* – received mixed reviews and had the lowest opening weekend of the series.

Nonetheless, the entire franchise has fared well, grossing over $3.3 billion worldwide.

~ ~ ~

However, for true movie buffs, there's more to see than a bunch of abandoned houses along Henry River. *The Hunger Games* films were shot at several locations in North Carolina and Georgia.

It's hard to pin down some scenes. The first *Hunger Games* movie was shot in towns like Asheville, Barnardsville, Black Mountain, Cedar Mountain, Charlotte, Concord, Hildebran, and Shelby.

The forest where Katniss spends time with Gale (Liam Hemsworth) was filmed in the Big Ivy Area, although most locals referred to it as the Coleman Boundary. A part of the Pisgah National Forest, you can find it on Route 197 near Barnardsville. With more than 30 miles of trails to hike, this mountain region contains some of the most rugged and scenic terrain in the state.

The woods and waterfalls of DuPont State Forest also provided a backdrop for many scenes. This is where Katniss discovers the wounded Peeta at the base of Triple Falls on Little River. You'll find the 10,400-acre forest in Henderson and Transylvania Counties, between the towns of Hendersonville and Brevard.

About 30 miles south of Hildebran, is the town of Shelby. A private warehouse west of South Lafayette Street was used for District 12's Hob, and for the Reaping Ceremony where the two Tributes are chosen by Effie Trinket (Elizabeth Banks). Commercial buildings alongside the railway tracks on South Morgan Street were transformed into District 12's scruffy industrial section.

The old Philip Morris Cabarrus Plant west of Concord, at 2321 Concord Parkway South, was used as a studio. Spanning 2,100 acres, and with 2.4-million square feet under one roof, it was used for scenes at the Capitol and the Tributes' training center, as well as for Districts 7 and 13.

The Tributes' grand entrance riding in chariots, where Katniss earns her the nickname "The Girl on Fire," was filmed in the Charlotte Convention Center at 501 South College Street in Charlotte.

Also in Charlotte, the Knight Theater at 430 South Tryon Street (part of the Blumenthal Performing Arts Center) was used for the pre-Game interviews conducted by flamboyant television presenter Caesar Flickerman (Stanley Tucci).

The survival games proper begin at the Cornucopia, which was built on private land alongside the North Fork Reservoir in Black Mountain. Being that the reservoir provides drinking water for the region, access to it is restricted, but you can view it from the Craggy Pinnacle Trail accessed at the Craggy Gardens Visitor Center, MM364 on the Blue Ridge Parkway.

The arena scenes were filmed on the outskirts of Wilmington, NC.

Other parts of the movies were staged in Atlanta, Georgia:

The mansion that served as President Snow's residence is really Swan House, better known as the Atlanta History Center. The address is 130 West Paces Ferry Road NW.

Sweetwater Creek State Park was used to provide the setting for District 13 in *Hunger Games: Mockingjay Part 1*. This is a peaceful tract of wilderness only minutes from downtown Atlanta. A tree-shaded trail follows the stream to the ruins of the New Manchester Manufacturing Company, a textile mill burned during the Civil War.

The hotel lobby of the Atlanta Marriott Marquis became the setting for the tribal quarters in *The Hunger Games: Catching Fire*. The 1663-room hotel is situated in downtown Atlanta at 265 Peachtree Center Avenue NE. While you're there, you can visit the nearby World of Coca-Cola. The soft drink was invented in Atlanta in 1886.

~ ~ ~

Want to visit District 12 like I did?

Henry River Mill Village is located at 4255 Henry River Road in Hickory, North Carolina. About halfway between Charlotte and Asheville, you will find the village 1 mile south of Hildebran on I-40 (Exit 119).

Walking along Henry River Road, my brother-in-law pointed out the row of dilapidated white clapboard houses that appear in *The Hunger Games*. One of them stood in for Katniss Everdeen's home. Then we fought our way through the underbrush to look at the river where the dam had been constructed. It was a sunny day, with none of the dismal feel you get in the movie.

Calvin Reyes is the current owner of Henry River Mill Village. In 2017, while looking for acreage for a family compound, he stumbled across the 72-acre plot. He stepped out into overgrown grass and surveyed the scene of a crumbling village. "It looked like a war zone," he says. "I immediately called my mother and said, 'I love this place. We have to buy it.'"

Reyes is moving forward with plans to transform the mill houses into overnight accommodations and restore the old country store as a restaurant and special event venue.

"We want to let people have a destination feel," said Reyes. "They'll be able to experience nature, culture, and history in a restorative project."

Tours are currently offered if you want a glimpse of the village. Proceeds from the tours go into the Henry River Preservation Fund.

Not only does the money go toward preserving history. It helps preserve a bit of movie magic.

CHAPTER 12
The Thomas Crown Affair

In 1968, I flew to Boston to attend the world premiere of *The Thomas Crown Affair*. A great heist movie starring Steve McQueen as a Boston millionaire who entertained himself by being gentleman thief. Being a film critic, I was invited by the studio to this gala gathering at a theater on Copley Square. So, there I was hanging out with "The King of Cool" Steve McQueen, chatting with erudite Paul Burke, and dining with a jovial Jack Weston.

Costume designer Theodora Van Runkle was at the premiere too, drawing attention in her see-through blouse.

Faye Dunaway couldn't make it.

Although McQueen was there to promote the movie, he only wanted to talk about racing cars. McQueen was a driver himself, although he often used the alias "Harvey Mushman" when participating in official races. A few years later, he would star in *Le Mans*, a film depicting a fictional 24 hours in France's famous Le Mans auto race. It features actual footage captured during the 1970 race. McQueen did much of his own stunt driving in *Le Mans*.

The Thomas Crown Affair was the first feature film written by Alan R. Trustman, a Boston lawyer and one-time banker. Trustman got the idea for the film while working at a bank and wrote the treatment after becoming a lawyer. He pitched the treatment to the William Morris Agency (now known as Endeavor). And WMA interested director Norman Jewison in the project.

The working titles for the film were *Thomas Crown, Esquire*; *The Crown Caper*; and *Thomas Crown and Company*.

Jewison and Trustman wanted Sean Connery for the part of Thomas Crown, but Connery was tired after completing *You Only Live Twice*, so he declined. Then, Jewison picked Rock Hudson for the role, but that didn't work out. Johnny Carson was even considered.

Steve McQueen lobbied hard for the part, but Jewison was reluctant to give it to him because he felt the role of a sophisticated Bostonian was too divergent from McQueen's rugged onscreen and offscreen personas.

But Jewison had successfully directed McQueen in 1965's *The Cincinnati Kid*, so he gave in.

~ ~ ~

Norman Jewison used a multiple screen technique for *The Thomas Crown Affair*, most notably during the first bank robbery. He became fascinated with multiple screens after seeing its use in Christopher Chapman's short film *A Place to Stand*, which had been exhibited at the 1967 Expo in Montreal.

One of *The Thomas Crown Affaire*'s most famous sequences is the chess match between Crown (McQueen) and Vicki (Dunaway), played in the study of Crown's mansion. The scene is played with very little dialogue, rapid cuts and a mixture of extreme close-ups and regular shots. The game depicted is based on an 1898 match in Vienna between Gustav Zeissl and Walter von Walthoffen. After Vicki defeats Crown, he suggests that they play something else, then kisses her.

Moviegoers praised the chemistry between McQueen and Dunaway. Critics liked Norman Jewison's stylish direction but considered the plotting and writing thin.

Roger Ebert called it "possibly the most under-plotted, underwritten, over-photographed film of the year." Nonetheless, it was one of the year's ten highest grossing movies.

McQueen, of course, performed his own stunts, which include playing polo and driving a dune buggy at high speed along the Massachusetts coastline.

~ ~ ~

The Thomas Crown Affair was filmed at over ninety locations in and around Boston during the summer of 1967. Most are easy to visit.

The Second Harrison Gray Otis House at 85 Mt. Vernon Street on Beacon Hill in Boston served as Thomas Crown's mansion. There are three houses named the Harrison Gray Otis House in Boston, each designed by noted architect Charles Bulfinch for Otis and his wife, Sally Foster Otis. Built in 1800-1802, this second of the three houses was a large, squarish three-story brick Federal-style mansion ornamented with Chinese fretwork balconies in iron. A historic district with narrow, gas-lit streets and brick sidewalks, you'll find it just north of Boston Common and the Boston Public Garden. The house itself is listed on the National Register of Historic Places.

The first robbery was filmed at what was then the Beverly National Bank (renamed Boston Mercantile Bank for the film), located at the North Beverly Plaza in Beverly, Massachusetts. Founded in 1802, it closed in 2010 after being acquired by Danversbank.

The second robbery was filmed at Brown Brothers Harriman, then located at 55 Congress Street, Boston. *BBH's* presence in Boston dates back to 1844. They manage approximately $66.4 billion in assets for their global client base.

The scene depicting a car theft was shot in downtown Beverly across from the City Hall. Just put 191 Cabot Street in your GPS.

The Mount Auburn Cemetery was used for the money-dumping scene. You can find it at Coolidge Avenue in Cambridge. Founded in 1831, it was the first rural or garden cemetery in the United States. Henry Wadsworth Longfellow (educator and poet), Oliver Wendell Holmes (author and poet), Julia Ward Howe (author and reformer), and Charles Sumner (abolitionist and U.S. senator) are among the notable people buried there.

Thomas and Vicki walked in the rain at Copp's Hill Burying Ground on Boston's North End. Located on a hill on which a windmill once stood, Copp's Hill was Boston's largest colonial cemetery. Dating from 1659, its notables include fire-and-brimstone preacher Cotton Mather; Robert Newman, the man who hung the lanterns on the night of Paul Revere's midnight ride; and Edmund Hartt, builder of the *USS Constitution*.

The polo sequences were filmed at the Myopia Hunt Club, 435 Bay Road in South Hampton. McQueen learned to play polo for the film, taught by pros Gary Wooten and Neil Ayer, with an assist by first assistant director Jack N. Reddish, who was a ranked player at the time.

The golf sequences were filmed at the Belmont Country Club, 181 Winter Street in Belmont, Massachusetts. Originally designed by Donald Ross in 1919, Belmont is ranked as one of the Top 100 courses in the US. In the movie, Steve McQueen is shown playing the 18th hole.

The glider scene was filmed in New Hampshire at the former Salem glider airport. Although Steve McQueen was in photographed in the cockpit on the ground, a local pilot actually flew the plane. If you want to visit it, the airport has been repurposed as Campbell's Scottish Highlands Golf Course at 79 Brady Avenue in Salem

The high-roller auction took place in the St. James Ballroom at the Eben Jordan Mansion, 46 Beacon Street on Beacon Hill. In the 1930s, the Italian Renaissance Revival townhouse became the headquarters for the Republican Women's Club. In the 1970s, it was acquired by the Unification Church. Recently, Mainsail Management bought the building from the church for $20.5 million.

In the movie, Thomas Crown drives his dune buggy wildly across Crane Beach in Ipswich, Massachusetts. With more than 1,200 acres of beachfront, dunes, and maritime forest, Crane Beach is visited by more than 350,000 people annually. In addition, it is among the world's most important nesting sites for piping plovers – a threatened bird that was nearly hunted to extinction for its eggs and feathers in the 19th century. Crane Beach has been recognized for its successful shorebird protection program. Motorized vehicles are prohibited on the beach except with special authorization.

Thomas and Vicki (McQueen and Dunaway) kiss at the top of Acorn Street, a narrow, cobblestone lane on Beacon Hill that is often called "the most photographed street in America."

Then there's the Marliave Restaurant, a rooftop dining area on Bosworth Street, where Vicki is shown surveillance photos of Thomas kissing another woman.

The old Boston Police Headquarters on Berkley Street has been renovated as the Loews Boston Hotel.

You can still jog along the footpath on the Boston side of the Charles River, between the Weeks Footbridge and the Anderson Bridge. Just like in the movie, the dome of Dunster House is visible in the background on the Cambridge side.

And you can spot Dulles International Airport, disguised with signage to make it look like a Boston airport.

Of course, you will recognize the Boston Common, the oldest city park in the United States. Some 50 acres in downtown Boston, the Common was used during the 1630s as a cow pasture. Then it was used for public hangings until 1817. The Common was used as a military camp by the British before the America Revolutionary War. It was formally converted into a public park during the 1830s. This iconic location served as a backdrop for several scenes in *The Thomas Crown Affair*.

Only the home of getaway driver Erwin (Jack Weston) was filmed in California.

Some say, Steve McQueen considered *The Thomas Crown Affair* the favorite of all his movies. Others say it was *Bullitt*. Both would qualify.

~ ~ ~

In 1999, MGM released a remake of the film, Directed by John McTiernan, the new version starred Pierce Brosnan as a millionaire art thief who is pursued by an insurance investigator played by Rene Russo. Faye Dunaway appeared in the 1999 film in a small role as Crown's analyst.

This adaptation is different from the original in that it is set in New York rather than Boston, and the robbery is of a priceless painting, a Monet, instead of cash.

I missed the premiere for the second go-round. But a reboot starring Michael B. Jordan is said to be in the works by Amazon Studios. If so, I'll try to attend that premiere ... wherever that might be.

CHAPTER 13
The Sheik

Your grandmother probably had a crush on Rudolph Valentino. A Hollywood sex symbol of the 1920s, he was known as "The Great Lover."

Although married twice, many sources hint that he was gay. Nonetheless, his handsome looks and romantic film persona made him the epitome of the Latin Lover.

Born in Italy, Rodolfo Pietro Filiberto Raffaello Guglielmi di Valentina d'Antonguella came to America in 1913. Unable to find steady work, he waited on tables and did gardening. Hired by a restaurant to dance the tango for $50 a week, he eventually became a taxi dancer at Maxim's Restaurant-Cabaret in New York.

Joining a traveling operetta and an Al Jolson stage show, he found his way to the West Coast. In Los Angeles, he continued teaching dance and built up a following of older women who would let him borrow their luxury cars. Sort of a gigolo, by some reports.

His first movie role was as an extra in *Alimony*. By 1919, he had carved out a career in bit parts. In 1921, his exotic looks scored him the lead in Metro's *The Four Horsemen of the Apocalypse*. It was one of the first films to make $1,000,000 at the box office, becoming the sixth-highest grossing silent film ever made.

Changing studios, he signed with Famous Players-Lasky (the forerunner of Paramount Pictures). Jesse L. Lasky cast him in *The Sheik*, a film that would cement his reputation as a leading silent movie star.

The plot: A charming Arabian *sheik* (Valentino) becomes infatuated with an adventurous, modern-thinking Englishwoman (Agnes Ayres) and abducts her to his home in the Saharan desert. She is kidnapped by a rival tribe, but the sheik rescues her. By then, they have fallen in love.

Playing the romantic role of Sheik Ahmed Ben Hassan, Valentino was hailed a major success.

The Sheik was shot on both coasts.

Part of it was filmed at Hollywood Beach in Oxnard, California. Oxnard became known as "Hollywood by the Sea." Famous for its golden sand and views of the Channel Islands, you can drive to

Oxnard, about 60 miles northwest of downtown Los Angeles, a little over an hour driving time.

The Guadalupe-Nipomo Dunes stood in for the North African desert. Fake palm trees were used to complete the look. The Guadalupe-Nipomo Dunes National Wildlife Refuge is located along an 18-mile-long coastal dunes landscape located about 99 miles northwest of Santa Barbara.

In Palm Springs, Tahquitz Canyon's waterfall provided a spectacular backdrop for the film. And the surrounding area subbed for the Sahara Desert. A popular resort city, Palm Springs is about 107 miles east of Los Angeles.

~ ~ ~

Back East, the Walking Dunes on the eastern tip of New York's Long Island became a desert landscape for *The Sheik*. The dunes get their name from the ever-shifting sand that has been described as a "slow-moving tsunami." At places, the dunes might reach 80 feet high. Sweet pepperbush and marsh grasses and sand slowly mix together as the dunes inch forward, moving inland at about 3 1/2 feet a year.

These dunes in Hither Hills State Park were fairly near the Famous Players Astoria Studios in Astoria, Queens, New York, where most of the shooting for *The Shiek* occurred.

Although called the Walking Dunes, walking on them is discouraged due to the dunes' delicate ecological nature. Don't tell anybody but I've strode barefoot across that rolling sand many times, back when I owned a beach house in nearby Montauk. If I close my eyes and concentrate, I can still feel the sand between my toes.

A ¾-mile trail leads you in a loop around the northernmost Walking Dune. A guide is available at the start of the trail at the end of Napeague Harbor Road.

~ ~ ~

Valentino's impetuous marriage to Jane Acker in 1919 was never consummated. Having married Valentino to break out of a lesbian menage a trois, she locked him out of the bedroom on their wedding night. This being what was termed a "lavender marriage," they didn't bother to divorce for four years.

By now a silent film heartthrob, Valentino became a frequent guest at The Palm Springs Hotel after it was purchased by the White sisters. A Scotsman, Dr. Welwood Murray, constructed and opened the Palm Springs Hotel in time for the great land auction of Nov. 1, 1887. The Palm Springs Hotel was a rambling one-floor ranch-style structure, capable of accommodating 26 guests. Dr. Florilla Mansfield White and her sister Cornelia Butler White purchased the hotel in 1913. Described as a "Desert Modernist Oasis," you can still find it at 2135 North

Palm Canyon Drive in Palm Springs, California. Surprisingly, the hotel has a Pressley Room, a Raquel Room, and a Sinatra Room, but no Valentino Room.

Cornelia White (she preferred to be called Miss Cordilla) was integral to Rudolph Valentino not being convicted in a crime of a scandalous nature. Here's the story: Valentino's eventual divorce decree with actress Jean Acker stated he could not remarry for one year, but Valentino's love for costume designer Natacha Rambova was not to be denied. In 1923 – one day before the year was up – they eloped to Mexico. Their honeymoon was spent at The Palm Springs Hotel, and somebody snitched. However, at trial, White testified that Rambova spent the night with *her* and not Valentino, who slept on the porch. Being that the marriage "wasn't consummated," Valentino was acquitted of bigamy.

In 1922, Valentino began filming *Blood and Sand*, portraying bullfighter Juan Gallardo. Having been led to believe the picture would be shot in Spain, he was bitterly disappointed to learn that the studio would be shooting it on a Hollywood back lot. He declared a "one-man strike" against Famous Players.

Unable to act due to the lawsuit, Valentino and Natacha Rambova went on a worldwide dance tour.

Eventually, Valentino signed a new contract with United Artists. Quite lucrative, it provided $10,000 a week for only three pictures a year, plus a percentage of his films. This was a time when the average American family barely made $2,000 *a year*. Considered disruptive, his wife was excluded from the film set by the contract, a term that caused a major rift in Valentino's marriage.

In August 1926, Valentino died from a bout of acute appendicitis, perforated ulcers and peritonitis. His early passing at the age of 31 caused mass hysteria among his fans.

His final film was the sequel *The Son of the Sheik*, which premiered nationwide shortly after his death.

~ ~ ~

My beach house in Montauk was only 18 miles from the Walking Dunes at Hither Hills. We liked to have popcorn shrimp and wine at The Clam Bar or grab a lobster roll at a place known as Lunch, both overlooking the dunes and the strip of sand that lines the Atlantic Ocean.

After a few glasses of pinot grigio, I could almost see Rudolph Valentino – the Shiek – on his grey Arabian stallion, galloping across the dunes that stood in for the Sahara Desert.

CHAPTER 14
Star Wars: The Force Awakens
Star Wars: The Last Jedi

Skellig Michael, an island off the coast of Ireland, was a perfect backdrop for the *Star Wars* sequel trilogy. Appearing in *Star Wars: The Force Awakens* (2015) and later in *Star Wars: The Last Jedi* (2017), the island is tucked away off the rugged coast of County Kerry, Ireland.

I've never set foot on Skellig Michael, although I've seen it from afar, while standing on the cliffs of the mainland.

Getting to Skellig Michael takes about 45 minutes by boat – but I turned down a ride. You see, it's listed among the world's most dangerous tourist attractions. Skellig Michael is a travel destination that might possibly kill you.

If you insist on going, fifteen boats travel the eight miles from Portmagee Marina on the Iveragh peninsula to Skellig Michael daily. The seas are usually rough, roiling like a teakettle. Only 180 people are allowed on the island each day. And you only get to spend two-and-a-half hours there.

If you're up to it, you can hike its 618 stairs, worn down by the steps of 14 centuries' worth of pilgrims, monks, Viking raiders, and visitors, to reach the top. The steps are very steep and uneven. There are no guardrails along the path, making the climb particularly dangerous.

If you are afraid of heights, pick some other way to spend the day.

The word "Skellig" derives from the old Irish word *sceillec*, which translates as "steep area of rock."

Skellig Michael rises 715 feet above sea level. Back in the 6th century, monks looking for an isolated place settled on the island. You can still see the monastery and beehive huts they built. Beehive huts (or clocháin) are circular dry-stone huts with domed roofs found mostly in Southwest Ireland.

By the 12th Century, the monks abandoned Skellig Michael due to the harsh conditions.

~ ~ ~

Filming on Skellig Michael began in September 2014 with scenes for *Star Wars: The Force Awakens*. The cast and crew returned to the island in September 2015 for *Star Wars: The Last Jedi*. In these movies, the island became the remote hideaway for Luke Skywalker. Its sharp, rocky cliffs and ancient stone steps instantly transported viewers to Ahch-To, the planet where Luke went into exile.

This rugged terrain was where Rey received her Jedi training. The crumbling stone huts of the early monks made a fitting setting for the ancient Jedi Temple where Rey embarks on her quest.

Due to the island's status as a protected site, crews could only film for a few hours each day. The harsh weather also tested the endurance of the actors. Daisy Ridley, who played Rey, remarked on how difficult it was to navigate the slippery stone steps in full costume, especially when the winds picked up.

Every May, fans gather on Skellig Michael with their lightsabers and costumes for a "May the Force be with you" festival.

~ ~ ~

In addition to the Island of Skellig Michael, *Star Wars: The Force Awakens* was filmed in several locations, including Pinewood Studios in England, the Rub' al Khali Desert in Abu Dhabi, and Iceland.

The Rub' al Khali (Empty Quarter) desert near Abu Dhabi doubled as the planet Jakku.

The snowy landscapes of Iceland, particularly around the Krafla Volcano and Myvatn Lake, were used for the setting of the Starkiller Base.

Also, Puzzlewood in the Forest of Dean in England was the setting for forest scenes on the planet of Takodana.

And a former airbase in Berkshire, England, was used to film the Rebel base on the planet D'Qar.

As for *Star Wars: The Last Jedi*, it was filmed at Pinewood Studio, in Croatia, and in Bolivia, as well as Ireland.

The Croatian city of Dubrovnik served as the setting for the city of Cano Bight.

And the ending battle scenes were shot in Bolivia at Salar de Uyuni, the world's largest salt flats.

As for the Irish locations, the Dingle Peninsula in County Kerry was used for the Jedi temple set. Brow Head in County Cork served as a location along with Loop Head, just north of Dingle. And some scenes of Ahch-To were filmed at Malin Head, the northernmost point of Ireland.

Puffins, the resident seabirds, provided unexpected cameos as Porgs in *The Last Jedi*. These little creatures provided some comic relief on screen and, off-screen.

I worked with several magazines that used a subscription fulfillment company that had offices in Limerick, Ireland. There was a branch office in Dingle, near Ireland's famous Cliffs of Moher. Many times, I flew over to inspect the operations, taking time to travel about the Republic of Ireland while I was there. My first impression was, "It really is green."

~ ~ ~

Lots of movies have been filmed in Ireland:

The Princess Bride was one of the first to feature the breathtaking Cliffs of Moher, (the "Cliffs of Insanity" in the fairytale movie.

While the actual invasion of D-Day took place in France, Steven Spielberg's Saving Private Ryan was filmed in the beaches of County Wexford.

Although William Wallace is a famous Scottish hero, the battle scenes of *Braveheart* were shot at Trim Castle in County Meath.

Kilmainham Gaol, a Dublin prison that once housed many of Ireland's rebels alongside thieves and bandits, was used as the backdrop for all jail scenes in *The Italian Job*.

Set in a fictional kingdom, *Ella Enchanted* was filmed in and around Dublin at Powerscourt Estate & Gardens, Luggala, and Kilruddy House.

Even the 2005 remake of *Lassie* – everybody's favorite dog story – was filmed in the Wicklow Mountains and in Dublin.

~ ~ ~

"In the end, Skellig Michael is more than just a *Star Wars* filming location – it's a symbol of Ireland's rich cultural tapestry and its lasting impact on both history and popular culture," says Skellig Island Tours.

If you're determined to stride the same mountainside as Luke and Rey, you can book a Landing Tour that allows you to get off the boat and explore the island. The tour departs from the Portmagee Marina in County Kerry. Landing tours begin in mid-May and wrap up at the end of September. Availability is limited, so you really need to reserve well in advance.

Along with *Star Wars: The Force Awakens* (2015) and later in *Star Wars: The Last Jedi* (2017), *Star Wars: The Rise of Skywalker* forms a so-called sequel trilogy.

Star Wars: The Rise of Skywalker was filmed primarily at Pinewood Studios in Buckinghamshire, England, and Wadi Rum, Jordan.

Ivinghoe Beacon, a scenic hill in England's Buckinghamshire, served as Kef Bir, an ocean moon in the Endor System.

The desert of Wadi Rum served as the fictional planet Pasaana.

Skellig Michael has also been featured in *Harry Potter and the Half-Blood Prince.*

Maybe next it could be a setting for Shakespeare's *The Tempest*. The Bard described the story as taking place "on a remote, magical island." Skellig Michael is certainly that.

CHAPTER 15

The Great Gatsby

The Jazz Age was known for its economic prosperity, flapper culture, shifting morals, rebellious youth, and the surreptitious speakeasies of Prohibition. That was the period F. Scott Fitzgerald captured like a time capsule in his masterpiece, *The Great Gatsby*.

Set in 1922, the book told the story of multi-millionaire Jay Gatsby who was still obsessed with a long-ago love, Daisy Buchanan. Reclusive, he hosts extravagant parties which he doesn't bother to attend. Taking place on Long Island's Gold Coast, Fitzgerald's novel centers on the uncrossable class divide between East Egg and West Egg – old and new money – separated by Long Island Sound.

"So we beat on, boats against the current, born back ceaselessly into the past," he wrote.

Jay Gatsby wants to move on, but he just can't escape his past.

Gatsby's whole life is this desperate attempt to recapture something that's gone, something he can never have back.

~ ~ ~

The first film version of *The Great Gatsby* was released in 1926. A silent drama, it starred Warner Baxer and Lois Wilson. A trailer is all that's known to exist. Fitzgerald's wife Zelda called it "rotten."

A second version hit screens in 1949, starring Alan Ladd and Betty Fields. Film scholar Wheeler Winston Dixon called it "a curiously tedious, flat, and unimaginative film."

The third one appeared in 1974. Directed by Jack Clayton, it starred Robert Redford and Mia Farrow. An IMDb review called it "vapid."

More recently, in 2013, *The Great Gatsby* was adapted to the screen by Baz Luhrmann. Leonardo DiCaprio as Gatsby, Carey Mulligan as Daisy, and Tobey Maguire as the narrator, Nick Carraway. Rotten Tomatoes says it's "a beautiful movie but not very deep."

Okay, none of them are perfect. Even F. Scott Fitzgerald's novel has been described by Goodreads as "a good book, though it is so ridiculously overrated."

But we're looking for movie locations, no literary criticism.

And since the version directed by Baz Luhrmann was mainly filmed in Sydney, Australia, we will focus on the 1974 Jack Clayton movie because its locations are within easy driving distance for most American readers.

~ ~ ~

Although the Fitzgerald novel takes place on Long Island's opulent North Shore, when it came time to film the 1974 movie version encroaching urbanization forced Paramount to look elsewhere for locations, settling for Rhode Island. A good choice, Newport offers an array of grand mansions to stand in for the fictional East Egg.

"During the Gilded Age of the late 19th century, Newport gained prominence as leaders of finance and industry from New York and elsewhere built ever-larger 'summer cottages' and enjoyed a glittering social life of dinners, sports and parties," explains the Preservation Society of Newport County. "Newport became the summer social capital of east coast USA."

Want to visit some of the sets?

The huge mansion where Jay Gatsby (Robert Redford) hosts his extravagant, jazz-age parties is found in Newport. Built in 1909 by the Oelrich family, Rosecliff was designed to be a "summer home suitable for entertaining on a grand scale." Seen at 548 Bellevue Avenue, the house was designed by architect Stanford White to be an imitation of the Grand Trianon retreat of Versailles, with a classical arcade of arched windows and paired columns. The house includes a grand ballroom and a swooping limestone "sweetheart staircase" that greets guests as they step inside.

Popular with moviemakers, Rosecliff also appears in Steven Spielberg's *Amistad*, in the rom-com *27 Dresses*, in the Harold Robbins automotive saga *The Betsy*, and in Arnold Schwarzenegger's *True Lies*.

The overwhelming gilt ballroom, where Gatsby (Redford) dons his old army uniform to dance with Daisy (Mia Farrow), is found in the Marble House at 596 Bellevue Avenue. Located just south of Rosecliff, it was built for the Vanderbilts.

If you're really interested in historic movie locations, you might want to take the Preservation Society of Newport County's tour that offers an inside look at 11 mansions and gardens.

The brief flashback to Gatsby and Daisy's first meeting was filmed at the white-pillared, Southern-style Linden Place Mansion. You'll find it waiting at 500 Hope Street in Bristol, about ten miles north of Newport off Route 114.

Scenes inside the Buchanans' home were filmed at Heatherden Hall, the grand Victorian house around which Pinewood Studios was built in Iver Heath at Buckinghamshire, England.

One driving scene was shot in Windsor Great Park in England, but other driving scenes took place in New York City and Uxbridge, Massachusetts.

Just south of the Queensboro Bridge's entrance, beneath the archway on 1st Avenue at East 59th Street in New York, is where Tom Buchanan (Bruce Dern) buys his mistress (Karen Black) a puppy.

Later, Tom and Daisy, along with Gatsby and ever-present Nick (Sam Waterson) arrive at the Plaza Hotel on Grand Army Plaza next to New York's Central Park. A French Renaissance chateau-style building, it has appeared in many movies – notably *Home Alone 2: Lost in New York* –back when it was owned by Donald Trump.

~ ~ ~

Som years back, my wife and I joined some friends for a picnic in Newport. We'd been to see Garrison Keillor perform his *Prairie Home Companion* radio show live at nearby Wolf Trap. We ate our *al fresco* lunch beneath the Old Stone Mill in Touro Park at the top of Mill Street in Newport. Some people say it's the ruins of an old stone windmill; others claim it's the remains of an ancient Viking tower.

Afterwards, we drove past many of the sites – like Rosecliff and Marble House – that are featured in the 1974 movie, *The Great Gatsby*.

As tour guide Chelsea Fernando put it: "Set against the rich social landscape of the Roaring Twenties, the film explores the decadence of the American dream and the nature of wealth and class division. The actors, draped in pastel seersucker, fine speckled cashmere, and silk ties and scarves in every color, played their roles against the backdrop of the gleaming white terracotta Rosecliff, standing in as Gatsby's grand Long Island estate. Rosecliff played its role perfectly."

The back lawn overlooks the Newport Cliff Walk and the Atlantic Ocean. We took a leisurely stroll, taking in the sights of the town from on high.

The last private resident of Rosecliff, J. Edgar Monroe, was known for his lavish parties, notable for being "relaxed and easygoing, with an air of conviviality uncommon in the social scene of the time" ... but perhaps more recognizable to Jay Gatsby.

~ ~ ~

But what of the real house that served as the model for Gatsby's fictional manse? Many on the north shore of Long Island – Great Neck being the town that Fitzgerald transformed into West Egg – vie for that honor.

Great Neck faces Cow Neck across the Manhasset Bay. This is where Fitzgerald placed Daisy Buchanan's residence with its infamous green light. The two points were "similar enough to confuse the gulls flying above."

Fitzgerald moved to Great Neck with his wife, Zelda, in the fall of 1922. Although Great Neck was the "less fashionable" of the two municipalities, researcher Gabrielle Lipton tells us, "it still abounded in the societal glitter Fitzgerald had long craved, not unlike the young Jay Gatsby."

The many candidates for Gatsby's house – or rather the inspiration for it – include Land's End, Harbor Hill, Oheka Castle, Winfield Hall, Beacon Towers, and Kings Point. Most of these locations probably informed Fitzgerald of the Gold Coast party scene – particularly Harbor Hill, which held a blow-out party in 1923 that featured a giant American flag made of light bulbs waving above the roof. Hating the title *The Great Gatsby*, Fitzgerald had wanted to name the book *Under the Red, White, and Blue*.

My favorite candidate for the Gatsby mansion is the Brickman estate in Kings Point, located at the end of what is now named Gatsby Lane. During Fitzgerald's time, it was owned by Richard Church of the Arm & Hammer Baking Soda family. Church threw huge Gatsby-esque summer parties, though it's unclear whether Fitzgerald was ever a guest. But it's documented that he lived nearby for about two years before going to France to finish writing his novel.

Set privately at the tip of the peninsula, the Brickman estate is one of the last remaining mid-19th-century North Shore mansions on Long Island. There is the mansion as well as nine other residential buildings. The main house features 8 bedrooms and 32 bathrooms with over 60,000 square feet of space. The grounds cover 60,000 square feet of gardens – as well as a koi pond, a pool, a terrace, and rolling lawns that encircle the property. With more than 1,600 feet of waterfront, it provides a spectacular panoramic view of the New York City skyline, Long Island Sound, and Manhasset Bay.

Land's End, a house once owned by Fitzgerald's acquaintance, a newspaper magnate named Herbert Bayard Swope, was bulldozed in 2011.

Harbor Hill was eventually demolished and the land developed into a modern housing development called "Country Estates." Some remnants of the estate – the gatehouse, the water tower, and the dairyman's cottage – are still standing and listed on the National Register of Historic Places.

Beacon Tower – once nicknamed "Cinderella's Castle – no longer exists. The main structure was destroyed in 1945, but remnants like the garden walls, gatehouse, and garage still exist. A new development was built on the site.

Over the years, Oheka Castle fell into disrepair and faced numerous arson attempts before being purchased and restored by real estate developer Gary Melius in the 1980s for $1.5 million. Today, it's a popular luxury hotel with 32 guest rooms and suites. You can stay there for about $335 a night.

Winfield Hall faced a sadder fate. Built in 1917 for retail magnate F.W. Woolworth, the mansion was badly damaged by a fire in 2015. Much deteriorated, the Glen Cove estate sold in sold in 2022 for a mere $8.25 million.

The so-called Gatsby Mansion at Kings Point has been described as "a formal manse sitting on the throne of the very tip of West Egg." The magnificent waterfront property at 26 Pond Road comes with over 8 acres of land. Gabrielle Lipton tells us, "The property continued to deteriorate until it was sold in April 2012 for much below its $39.5 million asking price."

Is this property the real inspiration for Fitzgerald's *The Great Gatsby* ... or merely a real estate agent's exaggeration? I don't know. Guess I'll have to drive out there and find out. (Editor's note: Suggest an estate named "Pembroke" was inspiration as Scott Fitzgerald rented a house just down the road in Glen Cove.)

CHAPTER 16
The Dark Knight

Following my years as publisher of Marvel Comics, I stepped across the aisle to consult with DC Comics. Mainly, I worked with Mad Magazine, I guess qualifying me as one of "the usual gang of idiots."

Just outside my office was a muscled mannequin of Batman. Clad in cowl and cape, the Dark Knight was an imposing figure. It always seemed like he was watching me.

Bill Finger, who co-created Batman with Bob Kane, is credited with many of the character's defining traits, including the "Dark Knight" nickname. But it was Frank Miller who reimaged Batman as a grim and gritty vigilante in *The Dark Knight Returns*.

Christopher Nolan made the description stick with his cinematic trilogy – *Batman Begins (2005), The Dark Knight (2008),* and *The Dark Knight Rises (2012)*.

The term "Dark Knight'" refers to Batman's "brooding, complex personality and his use of darkness and shadows as tools to fight crime."

As Lt. Gordon explains, "Because he's not a hero. He's a silent guardian; a watchful protector; a Dark Knight."

Christian Bale (as Bruce Wayne/Batman), Michael Caine (as Alfred Pennyworth), Gary Oldman (as Lt. James Gordon), Morgan Freeman (as inventor Lucius Fox), and Cillian Murphy (as Dr. Jonathan Crane/The Scarecrow) appeared in all three movies. Liam Neeson (as Ra's al Ghul, Batman's mentor) appeared in the first and last. Heath Ledger (as The Joker) won an Academy Award as Best Supporting Actor for his role as the supervillain.

Each of the three movies was a success in the box office: *The Dark Knight* was the number one grossing movie in 2008. *The Dark Knight Rises* was the third highest grossing movie of 2012. *Batman Begins* was the ninth highest grossing movie in 2005.

All three have racked in a worldwide box office approaching $2.5 billion. Not bad for movies about a crazed psycho in his Spandex underwear seeking revenge for the death of his parents.

~ ~ ~

Christopher Nolan depicted Gotham as an exaggeration of New York City, with elements taken from Chicago, the elevated freeways and monorails of Tokyo, and the walled city of Kalhoon in Hong Kong (which was the basis for the slum in the film known as The Narrows).

But the real locations? In *Batman Begins* and *The Dark Knight*, Gotham City was shot in Chicago. In *The Dark Knight Rises,* Gotham City was shot in Pittsburgh, New York City, and Los Angeles.

In October 2006, location scouting for Gotham City took place in the UK in Liverpool, Glasgow, and London, and in several cities in the US. Nolan chose Chicago for the first two movies because he "liked the area and believed it offered interesting architectural features without being as recognizable as locations in better-known cities such as New York City."

To give you locations you can visit, I have mostly picked places featured in *The Dark Knight*. After all, Chicago is a walkable city, allowing you to find them without having to crank up the ol' Batmobile.

But first things first:

> Wollaton Hall, an Elizabethan mansion in Nottingham, England — No, not in Chicago, Wollaton took on a very special role in when it appeared as Wayne Manor in *The Dark Knight* Trilogy. The Hall is five miles north of Gotham, Nottinghamshire from which Gotham City got its name. There, I

wanted to get that out of the way, before hitting the streets of Chicago.

Now we turn to the Windy City:

The destruction of Wayne Manor in *Batman Begins* provided an opportunity to move Wayne to a modern, sparse penthouse, reflecting his loneliness.

The lobby of One Illinois Center – This locale served as Wayne's new penthouse apartment. Bookcases were built to hide the elevators. The windows were covered with green screens allowing Gotham City visuals to be added later.

Wyndham Grand, 71 East Wacker Drive – The hotel's 39th Floor provides the views from Bruce Wayne's Penthouse. This is where the bedroom of Wayne's penthouse was filmed.

Chicago Post Office, 404 West Harrison – The first scene filmed in *The Dark Knight* was the bank heist. The robbery at Gotham National Bank by the Joker (Heath Ledger) was staged at the old Post Office. The exterior was shot at the northern corner at West Van Buren Street and Canal Street. A fake extension was built on the adjoining vacant lot.

Chicago Post Office (again) – This large disused building which occupies two blocks also stood in as the exterior of Gotham Police Department.

Parking Garage, 200 West Randolph Street – Batman rounds up the Scarecrow (Cillian Murphy) and other bad guys in this parking garage. Note: This is the same garage the Tumbler's rooftop chase took place in *Batman Begins*.

Richard J. Daley Center, Daley Plaza, Washington Street – Here is the headquarters of Wayne Enterprises. And yes, this is the plaza with the Picasso sculpture seen at the climax of *The Blues Brothers*.

Richard J. Daley Center, Daley Plaza, Washington Street – The center also houses the courtroom in which Harvey Dent (Aaron Eckhart) prosecutes the case against Falcone's successor, Maroni (Eric Roberts).

IBM Building, 330 North Wabash Avenue – This is the building that supplies the boardroom for Wayne Enterprises. A slab of black glass, on the north riverfront between Wabash and State Streets, the IBM building the provided multiple locations, including the offices of Harvey Dent, the Mayor, and the Police Commissioner.

McCormick Place, West Building, 2301 South Indiana Avenue – The vast warehouse of Wayne Enterprises' Applied Science Division, where Lucius Fox (Morgan Freeman) takes on the role of Batman's Q, is actually the Convention Hall of the West Building.

Chicago Theater, 175 North Street – Harvey Dent and Rachel Dawes go out for an evening at the ballet, only to find the performance cancelled – because Bruce Wayne has taken off on a cruise with the entire *corps de ballet*.

The Berghoff, 17 West Adams Street – Acting on a tip, Lt Gordon (Gary Oldman) arrests Sal Maroni (Eric Roberts) as he's enjoying a meal in the oak-paneled The Berghoff, a legendary German restaurant found between Dearborn and State Streets near the center of the Chicago Loop.

Illinois Center Buildings, 111 East Wacker Drive – A complex of five office buildings and a couple of hotels, this is where the fundraiser for Harvey Dent (Aaron Eckhart) is crashed by the Joker (Heath Ledger).

Willis Tower, 233 South Wacker Drive – With the decorative towers of the old Jewelers Building gone, in *The Dark Knight* Batman stares down into the dark city from the former Sears Tower.

Millennium Park Metra Station – The motorcycle-like Batpod emerges from below the city through the sinuously curving passageways of the Metra station.

Brach's Candy Factory, 401 North Cicero Avenue – This old structure stood in for Gotham General Hospital, blown up by the Joker. The building is no longer there, of course.

Lake Street between Wacker Drive and State Street – This stretch of roadway is where Bruce

Wayne (Christian Bale) takes to the streets in his Lamborghini. The Italian car company provided three cars – one of which was deliberately crashed.

Twin Anchors, 1665 North Sedgwick Street, Old Town – This is the bar where Harvey Dent/Two Face (Aaron Eckhart) shows up to have a word with corrupt Detective Wuertz (Ron Dean).

Navy Pier, 600 East Grand Avenue – As the Joker (Heath Ledger) wreaks havoc throughout Gotham City, panicky citizens begin to evacuate on ferries. This 3,300-foot pier was built in 1916 when Lake Michigan was used for commercial shipping. It fell into decline, until major renovations in 1976. Today, it encompasses over 50 acres of shops, restaurants, live theaters, family attractions, parks, gardens, and exhibition facilities.

As for the Batcave, that secret hideaway was filmed on a soundstage at Pinewood Studios in the UK. The "bat bunker" set (as it is now known) was designed to be large enough to hold any equipment the production might need – and so the cameras could film a full 360 degrees.

However, the entrance to the Batcave in the *Dark Knight Rises* was filmed 170 miles away at Henrhyd Falls in the Brecon Beacons, South Wales. The tallest waterfall in South Wales, Henrhyd was used as the external entrance to the Batcave.

Rotten Tomatoes calls *The Dark Knight* "dark, complex, and unforgettable." Heath Ledger received an Academy Award for Best Supporting Actor for his role as The Joker in *The Dark Knight*. Ledger died before the movie was released and the award was given posthumously.

"I'm whatever Gotham needs me to be," Batman says in *The Dark Knight*. Turning it around, Chicago proved to be whatever Chris Nolan needed it to be when filming there.

Go see for yourself, joker.

CHAPTER 17
Midnight in Paris

One year I decided to drive through Europe. I flew into Munich just in time for Oktoberfest, rented a car and drove through Austria, crossed the Alps through the Grand St. Bernard Tunnel, passed down the boot of Italy, cut over to Monaco, stopped off at St. Tropez to see some topless sunbathers (but it turned out to be a cloudy day), then veered over to see the prehistoric drawings in Cave Lascaux but that was closed to the public, so after overnighting it in the Medieval walled city of Carcassonne, I headed to Paris, stopping over at a little village known as Giverny. Having a degree in Fine Art, I knew Giverny was the home of the French Impressionist Claude Monet. This is where he painted those famous waterlily images.

Another thing: Giverny provided the backdrop for some of the opening scenes in Woody Allen's 48th movie, *Midnight in Paris*.

Paris and its environs have provided spectacular locales for many great movies – *Amélie*; *The Da Vinci Code*; *The 400 Blows*; *Breathless*; *Jules et Jim*; *Cleo de 5 à 7*; *A Man and a Woman*; *Thérèse and Isabelle*; *The Obscure Object of Desire*; *La Vie et Rose*; *Last Tango in Paris*; *Everyone Says I Love You*; *Is Paris Burning*; *Hugo*; *The Red Balloon*; *The Tall Blond Man With One Black Shoe*; *Les Misérables*; *Paris, je t'aime*; *Mrs. Harris Goes to Paris*; *An American in Paris*; and the list goes on!

But in Giverny I can't help thinking of Woody Allen's *Midnight in Paris*. The movie proper begins in Monet's Garden, where writer Gil Pender (Owen Wilson) reveals his love for the romantic image of old Paris. That sets the theme.

Monet lived on this estate from 1883 until his death in 1926. Monet's Garden provided a romantic scene on the famous Japanese-style wooden bridge that arches over Monet's lily pond

The village of Giverny is located on the river Seine at its confluence with the river Epte. About 50 miles northwest of Paris, you can visit Giverny as a day trip from the city.

Being in no hurry, I spent a few hours wandering around. There's plenty to see. Local attractions include the Museum of Impressionism Giverny, dedicated to the history of impressionism and the Giverny art colony.

There's also Hôtel Baudy. Once a humble roadside café, the little-known buvette evolved into a lively gathering place for artists after painter Claude Monet settled in the bucolic township. At the close of the nineteenth century, Paul Cézanne and Pierre-Auguste Renoir came here to paint the blossoms that flourish on the property. "Go to the Hotel Baudy in Giverny," Impressionist Camille Pissarro urged. "There you will find all that you need to paint, and the best company there is!"

Having lunch at Hôtel Baudy, I enjoyed a nice Gratine de Camembert and Gambas Grillees, along with an excellent Sauvignon.

~ ~ ~

I can't make up my mind which one of Woody's movies is my favorite. I think it's a tossup between *Manhattan* and *Midnight in Paris*.

Set in Paris, the film follows Gil Pender (Owen Wilson), a screenwriter and aspiring novelist, who is forced to confront his shaky relationship with his materialistic fiancée Inez (Rachel McAdams) when he begins magically traveling back in time to the 1920s each night at midnight.

Paris Insiders Guide puts it this way: "Woody Allen takes us on a wildly imaginative journey where we meet many of the famous writers, composers, and painters of the Jazz Age in Paris — Ernest

Hemingway, Scott and Zelda Fitzgerald, Cole Porter, Pablo Picasso, Salvador Dali, Gertrude Stein.

Woody Allen's *Midnight in Paris* elegantly captures the spirit of '20s and provides a glimpse into the marvelous and legendary *Belle Époque*.

But what does Gil learn? There in the past, he meets Henri de Toulouse-Lautrec, Paul Gauguin, and Edgar Degas, who all believes that the Renaissance was the best era in Paris. Gil comes to realize that everyone has his own opinion on which era should be considered the golden era versus the "dull" present.

~ ~ ~

Released in 2011, this romantic comedy-fantasy won an Academy Award for Best Original Screenplay. It was Woody's highest-grossing film ever, making $151 million worldwide on a modest $17 million budget.

So far, Woody Allen has won four Oscars – three Best Original Screenplays for *Annie Hall* (1977), *Hannah and Her Sisters* (1986), and *Midnight in Paris* (2011) — and a Best Director for *Annie Hall*. He has also won ten BAFTA awards, and two Golden Globes. *Midnight in Paris* won an Academy Award for Best Screenplay and was nominated for Best Picture, Best Director, and Best Art Direction.

So, in addition to Giverny, where did Woody Allen film *Midnight in Paris*?

Here are some locales that are easy to find:

The film starts with a dazzling selection of Paris locations and sets the scene at Hotel Le Bristol, one of the city's most luxurious hotels. Le Bristol serves as the Paris base for Gil, his fiancée Inez, and her parents. Located at 112 Rue du Faubourg Saint Honore, the hotel is smack in the center of the high fashion shopping district. You will find Pierre Cardin, Hermès, Lanvin, and Lacroix outlets within an easy stroll.

However, Rue Montagne Sainte-Geneviève has become the place to see in Paris for Woody Allen fans. These steps at the church of Saint-Etienne-du-Mont behind the Pantheon are where Gil goes nightly to catch his magic car ride into the past. You might call it the time portal of the movie.

Famous for its *Belle Époque* décor, Maxim's de Paris is one of the restaurants Gil and Adriana (Marion Cotillard) visit in the 1890s. Located at 3 Rue Royale, you too can dine there. But don't forget your wallet.

The movie features several great dining experiences. Among them, Le Grande Vefour at 17 Rue du Beaujolais; Le Polidor at 41 Rue Monsieur Le Prince; and Restaurant Paul at Rue Henri, Place Dauphine.

Hotel Le Meurice is the setting for the rooftop terrace wine tasting, where Paul (Michael Sheen) gives his famous wine tasting speech. Le Meurice has been awarded the Palace designation, the highest hotel rating in France. You can find it a 228 rue de Rivoli, if you're in the mood for an excellent glass of wine.

The garden of Musée Rodin provided the scene where Gil gets a tour by the museum director (played by Carla Bruni, the former First Lady of France). Musée Rodin is found at 79 rue de Varenne.

There are dozens of additional scenes set in locations that show off the city and environs.

For instance, Gil meets Gabrielle on Pont Alexandre III. One of most beautiful bridges in Paris, it connects the *Grand Palais* and *Petit Palais* on the Right Bank with *Hotel des Invalides* on the Left Bank.

Also, you will find Musée De L'orangerie at Place de la Concorde. You'll see it in the movie.

We also get a spectacular showing of Versailles. Located about 11 miles west of Paris, this sumptuous Palace and Gardens is the former royal residence commissioned by King Louis XIV.

On my way to Orly Airport, I stopped by Versailles and wandered through the Gardens with my camera, snapping pictures. Today, many of these photographs hang on a wall in my guest bedroom.

Inside the Palace, I was dazzled by the Hall of Mirrors, a grandiose Baroque-style gallery. The Hall and its adjoining salons were intended to illustrate the power of Louis XIV. The Treaty of Versailles was signed in this very room.

Midnight in Paris features scenes in the Hall of Mirrors, the most memorable showing noblemen running down the corridor. Other scenes took place inside Versailles's Salon de L'Oeil-de-Boeuf (Bull's Eye Salon). Seeing Versailles in person made me realize what a great tour the movie gives us.

After a few hours of strolling through the rooms of the magnificent Palace, I found my way to a small bistro across the street where I enjoyed a tasty Croque Monsieur with a delicious Bordeaux. Then I drove to the airport and caught a plane back to the States.

CHAPTER 10
The Stepford Wives

I used to live in Silvermine, an art colony in Connecticut. My neighbors included mystery writer Ed McBain (the pseudonym for Evan Hunter), *Saturday Review* editor Norman Cousins, social critic Vance Packard, and other literati. About 50 miles outside New York City, it is adjacent to Darien, Connecticut, an exclusive enclave that was once considered a "sundown town." Many maids and laborers are bused in from Stamford or Norwalk. In the movie *Auntie Mame*, liberal-minded Mame thumbs her nose at the town by endowing a Jewish children's home within the town limits.

Ira Levin wrote his satiric horror novel *The Stepford Wives* with Darien in mind. The movie *Gentleman's Agreement* was partially filmed here.

My friends in Darien jokingly referred to me as an "other element." But I was still invited to their Little League games, pizza nights, and family picnics.

Levin claimed he based the town of Stepford on nearby Wilton, Connecticut, where he lived in the 1960s. As he explained it, Wilton is a "step" away from Stamford, a major city 15 miles away.

But all my friends knew he had Darien in mind. When the movie version of his book was made, some of it was filmed at Darien's Goodwives Shopping Center.

Yes, you read that right – Goodwives Shopping Center.

I've had lunch there at the various restaurants, bought pinot grigio at the wine store, purchased brie at the cheese shop.

Last year, Darien did a little "cleanup," rebranding the shopping center as Old King's Market. The property is located at 25 Old Kings Highway North, near Goodwives River.

A spokesman for the shopping center issued a statement: "Many new and younger residents unfamiliar with the nearby river viewed the name 'Goodwives' negatively." The negative perception was exacerbated by its connection to *The Stepford Wives* – the shopping center served as a filming location for the movie.

See, I told you.

~ ~ ~

The Stepford Wives (1975) is the first movie based on Ira Levin's book. Directed by Bryan Forbes

(*Whistle Down the Wind*, *Séance on a Wet Afternoon*), it starred Katherine Ross and Peter Masterson as a couple – Joanna and Walter Eberhart – who move to exclusive Stepford, Connecticut. She makes friends with Bobbie (Paula Prentiss) but still doesn't feel a part of the community. All the other wives are too perfect.

To complicate matters, one of the town's leaders is a guy called Diz (Patrick O'Neal), who used to do audio-animatronics for the Disney theme parks. All the husbands belong to the mysterious Men's Association. The good wives are submissive.

The movie was remade in 2004, the second time starring Nicole Kidman and Matthew Broderick.

Same song, second verse.

Well, not quite. According to an industry insider: "The film was originally conceived as a darkly satirical piece with an ending closer to the finale of the original but negative results from test screenings caused Paramount to commission numerous rounds of reshoots which significantly altered the tone of the film and gave it a new ending."

A little "cleanup," that is.

Both movies made use of real locations. No exterior sets were constructed. The filmings took place in various towns in southern Connecticut – Darien, New Canaan, Westport, Redding, and Norwalk.

Drive around, you will recognize scenes from both.

While I prefer the original movie (full disclosure: Pete Masterson was a friend of mine), I'll list locations for both – places you can visit.

The 1975 version used several sites in the Greenfield Hill section of Fairfield, Connecticut.

Exteriors of the Eberharts' new house were filmed at 3455 Congress Street in Fairfield. However, the interiors were shot in a large Dutch colonial on Black Rock Turnpike in Redding. The high ceilings and large rooms perfectly accommodated all the cameras and bulky equipment.

Right across the street from the Fairfield house, you will find the Van Sant house at 3420 Congress. Carol and Ted Van Sant (Nanette Newman and Josef Sommer) are the Eberharts' oversexed neighbors.

At one point, Joanna and her friend Bobbie are shown strolling past the Greenfield Hill Congregational Church at 1045 Old Academy Road in Fairfield.

You can find the psychiatrist's house is at 367 Newton Turnpike in Weston, Connecticut.

The party scene was shot at 38 Langner Lane in Weston, Connecticut. There's still a pool in back.

Unfortunately, Daybreak Nurseries, originally located at 500 Main Street in Westport, is gone. The area has been redeveloped into housing.

One of the factories seen in the film was in fact a high school located at 23 Calvin Murphy Drive in Norwalk.

And, of course, many scenes were filmed at the Stop & Shop supermarket in the Goodwives Shopping Center in Darien (at the time it was a Grand Union).

You might note that the Eberharts' apartment before moving to Stepford was located at 325 West End Avenue in New York City.

The climax of the movie takes place at the Stepford Men's Association. That was filmed at the Lockwood-Mathews Mansion at 295 West Avenue in Norwalk, Connecticut. Now a museum, it was built in 1864-68 for railroad and banking magnate LeGrand Lockwood. It is open for tours.

~ ~ ~

The 2004 remake was filmed mainly in Darien, New Canaan, and Norwalk. A few scenes – like the Fourth of July fair – were shot at a Larger Cross Road estate in Bedminster (Lamington), New Jersey.

The CNN Studios at Columbus Circle in New York City passed as the workplace of Joanna Eberhart (this time Kidman). Turns out, she'd had a nervous breakdown, which is the reason the family moves to Stepford, a community where the wives "spend all day knitting, gardening, exercising, and caring for their homes in beautiful dresses."

"The true star of the movie is wealthy Connecticut," observes the CTMQ blog. "Most of the film, like the original, was shot in Darien, New Canaan, and Norwalk. The Stepford of 2004 is much wealthier than the 1975 version and the estates and mansions everyone lives in seem impossible. Well, impossible for people not familiar with Darien and New Canaan I guess."

Recently, a sprawling New Canaan estate at 62 Summersweet Lane, where director Frank Oz shot scenes for his remake of *The Stepford Wives*, went on the market for $6.9 million.

This time around there were bigger stars: Nicole Kidman, Matthew Broderick, Bette Midler, Glenn Close, Christopher Walken, even Faith Hill.

The creepy Men's Association was again shot at the Lockwood-Mathews Mansion in Norwalk.

You know the ending. Turns out, all the Stepford wives are robot replicas of the real wives.

I can't be sure, but I don't think my friends in Darien were robots. But these days, with AI, who can be sure?

CHAPTER 19

Jurassic Park

My mother invited me and my wife to join her and her friend Frank in Kaua'i, the northernmost populated island in the Hawaii archipelago. A landmass of 562.3 square miles, it is the fourth-largest of the Hawaiian Islands. The island is 33 miles long, 25 miles across at its widest point, but only 10 per cent of it is accessible by car.

Note: I spell Kauai as Kaua'i (the proper way) because I like being pretentious. But that's another story.

In 1778, British navigator James Cook discovered Kaua'i by accident while crossing the Pacific during his third voyage of exploration.

The island is 33 miles long, 25 miles across at its widest point, but only 10 per cent of it is accessible by car.

Kaua'i rises to about 5,200 feet above sea level, its highest point being Kawaikini Peak. But, in fact, the island is the top of an enormous volcano rising from the ocean floor.

Called the "Garden Isle," Kaua'i is the site of Waimea Canyon State Park and the Na Pali Coast State Park. Waimea is Hawaiian for "reddish water," a reference to the canyon's red soil. The erosion comes from rainfall on Mount Wai'ale'ale, one of the wettest places on earth.

Known as the Grand Canyon of the Pacific, Waimea Canyon is a large canyon approximately ten miles long and up to 3,000 feet deep, located on the western side of Kaua'i.

Waimea Canyon was used in the filming of the 1993 film *Jurassic Park*. It's 1997 sequel *The Lost World: Jurassic Park,* and the 2015 follow-up *Jurassic World* were shot in Kaua'i as well.

Jurassic Park's prologue, in which one of the park's staff falls prey to an unseen predator being loaded into a container, was filmed in Limahuli Gardens at Hanalei, on Kaua'i's northern coast. Located at 5-8291 Kuhio Highway, the garden is one of the properties comprising the National Tropical Botanical Garden.

Supposedly taking place in the Dominican Republic, the site of the Mano de Dios Amber Mine, where a lawyer (Martin Ferrero) decides that a paleontologist is needed on board, was also filmed on Kaua'i at Hoopii Falls on the eastern side of the island. These falls are located on public land, but it requires a short hike to reach the site.

The waterfront at Kapaa, on Kuhio Highway, was transformed into an outdoor cafe "in San Jose, Costa Rica." That's where Dennis Nedry (Wayne Knight) is involved with smuggling dinosaur embryos.

Your first view of Isla Nublar is really the green slopes of Kaua'i's Na Pali Coast as seen by helicopter. The best way to see this rugged landscape is either by boat or a helicopter tour. You'll find it just west of the Limahuli Gardens on the north shore.

The scene of the new arrivals encountering a Brachiosaurus by the lagoon was filmed at Puu Ka Ele Reservoir on the Jurassic Kahili Ranch, a working cattle ranch covering 2,500 acres south of Kuhio Highway near Kilauea, on the island's northeast tip. Its diverse terrain encompasses waterfalls, streams, and lush forests leading to more mountainous areas. Kahili has the distinction of having appeared in the first three *Jurassic Park* movies. Also, two of the sequels – *The Lost World* (1997) and Jurassic Park III (2001) –were filmed on the ranch's land.

The Jurassic Park Visitor Center was constructed at the Valley House Plantation Estate. You'll find it at 6191 Hauaala Road, Kealia, north of Kapaa. However, the interior scenes were filmed back in Los Angeles at the studio.

Located deep in the center of the island, at the base of Mount Wai'ale'ale, is the spot where the giant entry gates to "Jurassic Park" were erected. Although the gates were removed after filming, two tall poles remain on either side of the path. A tough place to visit, it requires an eight-mile hike, following Kuamo'o Road from Wailua until it changes from a paved road to a dirt track, finally becoming the Waikoko Forest Management Road.

The spot where Grant (Sam Neill) stumbles across the raptor nest is on another of the National Tropical Botanical Garden properties. He finds the hatched eggs beneath the giant fig trees at the Allerton Gardens, 4425 Lawai Road, Koloa.

In *The Lost World*, the beach where the unfortunate family decides to hold a picnic is Kipu Kai Beach, on Kaua'i's south shore. It's only accessible by boat.

A couple of miles to the northeast you'll find Pilaa Beach, where the military comes ashore to save the day. A rarely visited beach, it's not ideal for swimming due to the rocky ocean bottom and rip tides.

The iconic waterfall featured in the background scenes of *Jurassic Park* is Manawaiopuna Falls (also known as "Jurassic Falls"). Located in Hanapepe Valley on west side of the island, this waterfall is approximately 400 feet high. It's only accessible by helicopter.

Manawaiopuna Falls is private property owned by the Robinson Family. Only Island Helicopters Kauai has permission to land and visit the falls. The helicopter pad built for the movie has since been washed away. The 55-minute helicopter rides cost about $250 per person.

Jurassic Park's director Steven Spielberg was no stranger to Kaua'i, being that the opening scene of *Raiders of the Lost Ark* was filmed on the island in 1980.

~ ~ ~

Secret Falls – you'll need a guide for this one. To access this hidden waterfall, head to the Lower Wailua River where you will need to rent a kayak or sign on for a guided tour to take you to the falls. This is a half-day adventure.

Even though Frank was in his 80s, he outdid me when it came to paddling a kayak. I had to huff and puff to keep up.

After kayaking 4 miles, you reach the trailhead. There you will beach your kayak and continue on foot. The distance to Secret Falls is about 1 mile. The trail winds its way through incredibly lush tropical foliage, including wild ginger, tropical mangos, gigantic ferns, and elephant grass too high to see over. What looks like saplings surrounding you are actually the roots of larger trees.

This 45-minute hike can be quite muddy. This route includes stream crossings up to waist deep and a gain of 465 feet in elevation. When dry, it's only a low-difficulty hike, but it becomes moderately challenging if it has rained recently. That's when the trail becomes muddy and slick. And since this area is a tropical rainforest, it rains frequently!

Once you reach the falls, you'll agree the journey was totally worth the effort. Uluwehi Falls (its official name) plunges 120 feet over a spectacular cliff into the lovely pool below. A refreshing swim is one of the hike's highlights. Feel free to jump in!

We went in, clothes and all. It felt good after the sweaty hike.

Afterward, we enjoyed a picnic on the rocks. My mother had backed a light lunch. We invited our guide to join us. He said *"Mahalo!"* as he chowed down. I learned that was Hawaiian for "Thank you!"

I even learned the word *"Ho'olohi!"* to shout at Frank as we paddled our kayaks back to the base, me huffing and puffing all the way. That translated as "Slow down!"

~ ~ ~

The first movie made on Kaua'i dates back to 1934. *White Heat* was a tale of "racial prejudice and miscegenation on a Hawaiian sugar plantation.".

Lois Weber – a silent film director often compared to D.W. Griffith – spent five weeks filming on the plantations of the Kekaha Sugar Company and the Waimea Sugar Company and at Alexander McBryde's Lawai Kai estate. Now considered lost, *White Heat* (working title: *Cane Fire*) was Weber's first talkie (and, as it turned out, her last picture).

Other films shot on the island include *Raiders of the Lost Ark* (1981), *Pirates of the Caribbean: On Stranger Tides* (2011), *King Kong* (1976), *Mighty Joe Young* (1998), *George of the Jungle* (1997), *Soul Surfer* (2011), *The Descendants* (2011), *Outbreak* (1996), *Tropic Thunder* (2008), *Hook* (1991), *Six Days/Seven Nights* (1998), *Blue Hawaii* (1961), *South Pacific* (1958), and, of course, *Jurassic Park* (1993), *The Lost World: Jurassic Park* (1997), and *Jurassic World* (2015).

Even some animated films drew inspiration from Kaua'i. *Lilo & Stitch* (2002) and *Avatar* (2009) come to mind.

Yes, you can experience a "Jurassic Park" theme park at Universal's Islands of Adventure in Orlando, Florida, and at Universal Studios Hollywood. There you can encounter dinosaurs and ride themed attractions.

The ride was built while the film was still in production and opened at Universal Studios Hollywood on June 21, 1996. Duplicates of the ride have since been built at Islands of Adventure and Universal Studios Japan.

Just for the record, I didn't see any dinosaurs on Kaua'i.

CHAPTER 20

Ghostbusters

I lived in New York City for nearly 25 years. In all that time, I never saw a ghost. But if you take the movie *Ghostbusters* at face value, the Big Apple is teeming with ectoplasmic entities.

Who you gonna call?

I'd call a cab to ferry me around the City looking at locations where the comedy classic was filmed.

Ghostbusters (1984) is a film directed by Irvan Reitman (*Meatballs, Stripes, Kindergarten Cop*) and written by Dan Aykroyd and Harold Ramis. It tells the story of three eccentric Columbia University parapsychology professors who set up a service called Ghostbusters, kind of like an Orkin for ghosts. They have developed high-tech nuclear-powered equipment to capture and contain ghosts, demons, and otherworldly invaders.

Right off, they get called to the apartment of a woman with a demon in her refrigerator. But when she and a neighbor get possessed, the Ghostbusters have a problem on their hands. Matters get worse when an Environmental Protection Agency inspector has them arrested. But the trio (and their new assistant) come to New York City's rescue when a gigantic Stay Puff Marshmallow Man starts wreaking havoc. By crossing their proton energy streams, they banish this shapeshifting god of destruction back to his own dimension, becoming heroes.

Roadtrippers tells us: "As the titular ghostbusters, Dr. Peter Venkman (Bill Murray), Dr. Ray Stantz (Dan Aykroyd), Egon Spengler (Harold Ramis), and later Winston Zeddemore (Ernie Hudson) don proton packs and drive their ectomobile uptown, downtown, and anywhere else they're summoned." Sigourney Weaver and Rick Moranis co-star as the neighbors who get possessed. And William Atherton is the officious EPA inspector.

Ghostbusters was inspired by Dan Aykroyd's fascination with the paranormal. You might say it was in his blood. His father wrote a book titled *A History of Ghosts.* His mother claimed to have seen ghosts. His grandfather experimented with high-vibration crystal radios to contact the dead. And his great-grandfather was a famous spiritualist.

Aykroyd's idea was to make a comedy about ghosts in the style of an old Abbott and Costello movie.

Ghostbusters was a hit, to date raking in over $370 million worldwide.

Movie critic Peter Travers called it "wonderful summer nonsense." Roger Ebert gave it 3 ½ stars out of 4. Arthur Knight snobbily said it had "far more style and finesse" than you would expect from the creative team behind *Meatballs* and *Animal House*.

With this kind of success, it launched a franchise comprised of five movies so far – the original *Ghostbusters* (1984), *Ghostbusters II* (1989), *Ghostbusters: Afterlife* (2021), *Ghostbusters: Spirits Unleashed* (2022–2023), and *Ghostbusters: Frozen Empire* (2024).

Reboots include *Ghostbusters* (2016). *Ghostbusters: Answer the Call* (2017–2018), and *Ghostbusters Crossing Over* (2018).

Add two television series – *The Real Ghostbusters* (1986-1991) and *Extreme Ghostbusters* (1997). Not to mention video games and the like.

~ ~ ~

I was reminded of *Ghostbusters* when walking in New York's Tribecca neighborhood, heading to Robert De Niro's restaurant, I spotted a familiar looking firehouse at 14 North Moore Street. It was the Ghostbusters headquarters!

Well, at least in the movie.

In reality, this is Hook & Ladder Company 8, an active New York City Fire Department station. Built in 1903, this narrow stone building is recognizable by it arched red door.

Hook & Ladder Company 8 offers a great photo op. I recommend taking the 1 subway to the Franklin Street stop, seeing the Ghostbusters HQ building, then walking to Chinatown or Little Italy for some eats.

Other *Ghostbusters* locations?

The movie was filmed in New York City and at the Warner Bros. Burbank Studios in Los Angeles,

Spook Central was shot at 55 Central Park West, a 19-floor co-op on the Upper West Side. In real life, this apartment has been home to Ginger Rogers, Calvin Klein, and music mogul David Geffen. In the movie, it's the apartment of cellist Dana Barrett (Sigourney Weaver) and the Cult of Gozer. Turns out, Barrett's fridge is a portal to another dimension.

The church that the Stay Puff Marshmallow Man steps on is the Holy Trinity Lutheran Church next door to 55 Central Park West.

Another location is Tavern on the Green, a legendary restaurant in Central Park. It was recognizable by its trees wrapped with twinkling white lights.), Accountant Louis Tully (Rick Moranis) is chased there by a red-eyed demon he mistakes for a bear. A former sheepfold next to Sheep Meadow, Tavern on the Green opened as a restaurant in 1934.

Another landmark you might recognize is Lincoln Center. Venkman (Bill Murray) meets Barrett (Sigourney Weaver) as she's leaving orchestra rehearsal there. As they walk around the fountain in the center of Josie Robertson Plaza, he tells her that there's been a break in her case – and asks her out on a date. Located between West 65th and 62nd streets and Columbus and Amsterdam avenues on Manhattan's Upper West Side, the performing arts complex is home to the Metropolitan Opera, the New York City Ballet, and the New York Philharmonic.

You'll also want to check out Columbus Circle, where the Stay Puff Marshmallow Man was first spotted.

Other scenes took place on the Columbia University campus. That's where the dean informs the boys that the Board of Regents has decided to terminate their grant. Fact is, there is no real Weaver Hall (or Department of Paranormal Studies) at Columbia University, but the Low Memorial Library where Venkman and Stantz hatch their business plan is located at West 116th Street between Broadway and Amsterdam avenues.

Also, you'll want to sit on the steps (between the lions) at the New York Public Library on Fifth Avenue at 42nd Street. That location was used in the movie's opening scenes. When Venkman and Stanz arrive at the Library, they find Spengler beginning his investigation of the Rose Main Reading Room.

The loan office scene where the Ghostbusters beg for a business loan was filmed at the US Manhattan City Bank at 489 Fifth Avenue, just across the street from the New York Public Library.

~ ~ ~

For some of the other scenes you would have to fly to L.A.

The Sedgewick Hotel where we first see the green Slimer ghost is located in New York in the movie, but the filming took place at the Millennium Biltmore Hotel at 506 Grand Avenue in Los Angeles.

Another non-Big Apple location is Val's Restaurant at 10130 Riverside Drive in Toluca Lake, California.

Down in the library's basement, Venkman looks at the symmetrical tower of books and says, "No human being would stack books like this." He's right. This is where he finds lots of ectoplasmic residue – and a very scary apparition. Rather than the New York Public Library, the haunted stacks were filmed across the continent inside the Los Angeles Central Library at 630 West 5th Street in downtown Los Angeles.

Not appearing in the movie but talked about is Camp Wokanda. Ray reminisces about going there as a boy and roasting Stay Puff marshmallows over

Dirty Dancing In An Ice Storm

the fire. Well, there actually is a Camp Wokanda, but it's found at 1125 West Lake Avenue in Peoria, Illinois.

The Ecto-1 ectomobile was built from a 1959 Cadillac Miller-Meteor ambulance retro-fitted with ghost-catching gadgets. A modified leopard snarl was used for the siren sound. The vehicle finally broke down on the last day of filming.

The Slimer ghost was called Onion Head during the filming. Aykroyd's inspiration for Slimer was his late friend John Belushi. Belushi was supposed to play Venkman, but when he unexpectedly died from a drug overdose, Bill Murray stepped into the role without even having a contract.

~ ~ ~

Standing outside Hook & Ladder Company 8, I was determined to get a look inside. But short of calling in a fire, I didn't know how to get past those iconic red doors. Just then, fate intervened and the doors swung open, responding to a two-alarm fire (honest, I didn't do anything). Stepping aside, I peered into the firehouse as the screaming red truck zoomed out.

But I didn't recognize anything. As I later learned, the interior scenes in *Ghostbusters* were filmed at Old Fire Station 23 in Los Angeles.

CHAPTER 21
The Shining

We all know that the Overlook Hotel in Stanley Kubrick's *The Shining* is found in Colorado. After all, Stephen King's novel on which the film is based told us so – right?

Well, it did.

But it's not.

After writing *Carrie* and *'Salem's Lot*, both of which are set in small towns in Stephen King's native Maine, he was looking for a new setting for his next book: "I wanted to spend a year away from Maine so that my next novel would have a different sort of background," King explains. So, he opened an atlas of the United States on his kitchen table and randomly pointed to a map. His finger landed on Boulder, Colorado.

Ironically, only one brief scene in the entire 2-hour 26-minute movie was filmed in Colorado. Most of *The Shining* was filmed on a sound stage in England.

~ ~ ~

Published in 1977, *The Shining* was King's third novel. The story centers on Jack Torrance, a struggling writer and recovering alcoholic who takes a job as the winter caretaker at the Overlook Hotel in the Colorado Rockies. His family accompanies him on this job, including his young son, Danny, who possesses "the shining," a psychic ability that allow the child to glimpse the hotel's horrific true nature.

It was inspired by King's real-life visit in 1974 to the Stanley Hotel in Estes Park, Colorado. "When we arrived, they were just getting ready to close for the season, and we found ourselves the only guests in the place — with all those long, empty corridors" He stayed in room 217 (not 237 as depicted in the movie).

Years earlier, King had started a novel about a psychic boy in a psychic amusement park, but he abandoned the idea. During the night at the Stanley, this story came back to him.

"That night I dreamed of my three-year-old son running through the corridors, looking back over his shoulder, eyes wide, screaming. He was being chased by a fire-hose," King recalls. "I woke up with a tremendous jerk, sweating all over, within an inch of falling out of bed. I got up, lit a cigarette, sat in a chair looking out the window at the Rockies, and by the time the cigarette was done, I had the bones of the book firmly set in my mind".

King has said his personal struggle with alcoholism and other experiences influenced the characters and themes of the novel.

The Stanley Hotel is known for its spooky reputation and has become a popular tourist destination for fans of "The Shining".

King's editor at Doubleday tried to talk him out of *The Shining* because he thought that after writing *Carrie* and *'Salem's Lot* he would get typecast as a horror writer. King considered that a compliment.

The novel was King's first hardcover bestseller, its success establishing him as "a preeminent author in the horror genre."

~ ~ ~

The Shining was the second Stephen King novel to be adapted for the screen. Directed by Stanley Kubrick, the 1980 film stars Jack Nicholson, as scary Jack Torrance, Shelley Duvall as his hysteric wife Wendy, and young Danny Lloyd as their psychic son Danny. The family spends five wintry months in an isolated hotel in the mountains of Colorado – which turns into a struggle between Jack and the evil hotel.

The ultimate haunted house story.

The Shining is considered one of the greatest horror films ever made. Even so, Stephen King hated Kubrick's adaptation of his novel. His disdain comes down to the most significant distinction between the book and movie: the Overlook Hotel's motivation for causing Jack's madness and the Overlook's intended victim.

Kubrick's adaptation left the main characters and plot points intact. Both versions include Jack Torrance as a recovering alcoholic who seeks to use his time at the Overlook to work on his writing. In the movie, the hotel drives Jack mad. However, in the novel, Danny is the Overlook's intended victim, and Jack is merely a way for the evil hotel to get to him. The Overlook wants Danny dead so it can absorb his "shining" ability to fuel its dark energy. In the movie, the Overlook's motive isn't quite as clear, seemingly targeting Jack as a weak vessel whose soul can easily be corrupted.

"Kubrick was known for his meticulously crafted shots, and *The Shining* is no exception," notes the Giggster movie guide. "Every frame of the film is loaded with meaning, from the sweeping aerial shots of the Overlook Hotel to the tight close-ups of Jack Nicholson's increasingly crazed face."

Kubrick's *The Shining* has significantly influenced pop culture. The iconic "Here's Johnny!" scene has been referenced about a zillion times. The quote ranks #68 in the American Film Institute's 100 Years ... 100 Best Quotes list.

~ ~ ~

Still not scared? Then you may want to visit the places seen in the movie. Many of the filming locations still exist and can be visited, with some even becoming popular tourist attractions.

However, many of the scenes in the movie do not take place where you think they do.

For instance, the opening scene with the Torrences' car winding along a colorful mountain road on its way to Overlook Hotel was actually shot in Montana. You will see Saint Mary Lake and Goose Island as part of the scrolling landscape. The scenery shifts from Douglas firs and Ponderosa pines to snowy landscapes as a helicopter camera tracks the car along the Going-to-the-Sun Road in Glacier National Park. You can make the same drive yourself.

For the establishing shots of the Overlook Hotel, the movie features the front of Timberline Lodge, a historic hotel located on the south face of Mount Hood in Mount Hood National Forest, Clackamas County, Oregon. You can find it for yourself just off Timberline Highway, which runs parallel to Highway 26, and can be accessed via West Leg Road.

No, the Timberline doesn't resemble the Colorado-based Stanley Hotel in the least. Built in the 1930s, the Timberline was designed by Gilbert Stanley Underwood, the same architect who did the Ahwahnee Hotel in Yosemite Valley, California. The

Ahwahnee served as the model for the interiors of the Overlook in the movie, but nothing was filmed on location at the Ahwahnee. Most of the interiors of the Overlook Hotel were filmed at Elstree Studios in Borehamwood, England.

The Gold Room, where Jack is served by a taciturn bartender, was based on King's own experience at the Stanley Hotel. After dinner, his wife decided to turn in, but he took a walk around the empty hotel, ending up in the bar where he was served drinks by a bartender named Grady. The Gold Room was filmed on Stage 5 at Elstree Studios. Despite rumors, pick-up shots for the bar were not filmed in the cabaret room of American Legion Hollywood Post 43 in Los Angeles.

The movie changed Room 217 from the book to Room 237. One of the reasons for this is that the owners of the real hotel were afraid that guests would avoid Room 217 after seeing it used in the film – and there was no Room 237 in the Timberline Lodge. (In reality, Room 217 became the most-requested room at the Timberline due to its pop culture significance.)

A hedge maze plays a significant role in the movie, representing both the characters' physical and psychological disorientation. However, this maze was not included in Stephen King's original novel, which instead featured animal topiary that comes to life. Also, there was no maze at the Stanley Hotel, the original inspiration for the Overlook – though there is one there now (inspired by the movie). No maze existed at the Timberline Lodge or the Ahwahnee Hotel either.

In fact, the "maze" seen in *The Shining* was never a real maze anywhere. The maze in the film was created on the backlot of the MGM Borehamwood Studios in England. The overhead shot of the maze was filmed (using a matte painting) in the parking lot of the Canterberry Building at Borehamwood. And the maze at night was filmed on Stage 1 at England's Elstree Studios. A section of hedge at Radlett aerodrome provided the maze seen in the summer sequences.

There's an exterior road scene in *The Shining* where Dick Halloran is trying to drive to the Overlook and hits a traffic jam caused by an overturned truck hat smashed into a red Volkswagen. This part of the movie was filmed on the Radlett Aerodrome outside of London.

Despite being an American filmmaker, Stanley Kubrick spent most of his life in England, and shot all his later films there, regardless of whether they took place in New York City, Vietnam, or, in the case of *The Shining*, the Rocky Mountains of Colorado.

Almost any time a character is indoors in *The Shining*, they were actually on a soundstage in England. Scenes shot at Elstree Studios include the interiors of the Torrance's Boulder apartment, Dick Halloran's place in Miami, the ranger station, and Durkin's Store.

The Record for the Most Retakes of a Dialogue Scene: Kubrick shot the scene between Danny (Danny Lloyd) and Dick Halloran (Scatman Crothers), during which Dick describes the Shining to him, a whopping 148 times. Kubrick was a perfectionist.

Before Jack gets the job as the winter caretaker of the Overlook, the Torrance family lived in an apartment in Stovington, Vermont. While the interior scenes of that apartment were filmed on a set built at Elstree Studios, the exterior establishing shot was an actual apartment complex in Boulder, Colorado. You can see the Kensington Apartments for yourself at 2950 Bixby Lane, Boulder, Colorado. No need to drive all way to Vermont.

Kubrick's adaptation was a deliberate departure from traditional horror tropes. It focused on the psychological descent into madness and the ambiguity of the supernatural, rather than relying on jump scares or overt gore.

Many Stephen King fans felt the film was a disappointment, while others praised Kubrick's vision.

~ ~ ~

For diehard fans, the most appealing place to visit is the Stanley Hotel. That hotel, being the inspiration for King's story, has fully leaned into this reputation by hosting The Shining Tour. You can even stay at the Stanley.

Timberline Lodge, where many of the exterior locations of *The Shining* were filmed, is also open to the public, though it doesn't seem to offer an experience catering to fans in the same way that the Stanley Hotel does.

Unfortunately, there aren't any tours available of Elstree Studios in the UK, and many of the sets used in *The Shining* no longer exist.

Thank goodness the evil Overlook Hotel does not really exist!

CHAPTER 22

La La Land

Being an editor and filmmaker, my son Kevin lives (of course) in North Hollywood. The eco-friendly house where he and his partner Clarise reside is only a few blocks from the Burbank line. Just around the corner is the building which served as the nightclub in the Oscar-winning movie *La La Land*.

From there, you can see the famous HOLLYWOOD sign on Mount Lee in the Hollywood Hills. It used to read HOLLYWOODLAND before part of it collapsed in 1949.

North Hollywood was once part of the vast land holdings of the Mission San Fernado Rey de España. The district was established by the Lankershim Ranch Land and Water Company in 1887. First named "Toluca," then "Lankershim," it was renamed "North Hollywood" in 1927.

Neighboring Burbank was named after a sheep rancher. Today, this city in the southeastern end of the San Fernando Valley in Los Angels is home to numerous media and entertainment companies.

La La Land is the nickname for Los Angeles. It emerged in the late 1970s and early '80s, playing on the city's initials (L.A.) and referencing its reputation "as a place of dreams, sometimes unrealistic, in the entertainment industry."

So, when director Damien Chazelle (*Whiplash, Babylon*) decided to make a musical romance about Hollywoodland, he chose the title that encapsulates all the hopes and dreams and disappointments that describe it so well – La La Land.

La La Land (2016) has been described as "a glorious, daring, romantic, old-school song-and-dance production with a melancholy twist." As one fan observed, "*La La Land* is not a story, but rather an ode to Hollywood."

The movie follows two ambitious dreamers: Mia, an aspiring actress (played by Emma Stone) and Sebastian, a jazz pianist (played by Ryan Gosling). As W Magazine describes it, "Their love affair, with all of its ups and downs, is set in Los Angeles, which is less a backdrop than a vast and intriguing third character."

"At first, I thought L.A. was really bizarre," Damien Chazelle says. "But L.A. is full of surprising secrets. In *La La Land*, I tried to show everything that is uniquely L.A.: the weird infinity roads, the alleys, the toothpick palm trees, the open horizon, and the big sky. So even if you turned off the sound, you would know that the movie was set in L.A."

A big fan, Konark Panday sums up the movie's plot like this:

> Boy Meets Girl, Girl Meets Boy.
>
> Boy loves the Girl. Girl loves the Boy.
>
> Boy inspires the Girl to seek her own identity. Girl inspires the Boy to seek his own tune.
>
> Boy follows his passion and finds success. Girl follows her passion and finds success.
>
> Boy's love for the Girl lives through his passion and her inspiration. Girl's love for the Boy lives through her passion and his inspiration.
>
> But they do not end up together. And that is okay.
>
> La La Land is not a celebration of Romance (the happiness of finding your partner, or the grief of letting them go).
>
> La La Land is a contentment of the Irony of Love. It shares what could have been versus what is ! And whatever is, is okay; no matter how beautiful what could have been would have been.

At the beginning of the movie, Emma Stone's character is all about paying the bills, while Ryan Gosling's character is about following his passion. Then, somewhere in the middle of the movie, they switch. And we can identify with both of them – the "artist" who compromised his artistic integrity, and the "realist" who began to follow her dreams.

La La Land was nominated for 14 Academy Awards, winning six including Best Director. At age 32, Damien Chazelle became the youngest person to have won an Oscar as Best Director.

Although filmmaking was Chazelle's first love, he'd struggled hard to make it as a jazz drummer before accepting that he didn't have the talent. Nonetheless, that experience paid off in the making of both *Whiplash* and *La La Land*. "I can't remember a time that I didn't want to write and direct films," he says.

Thanks to the success of *Whiplash*, he was able to attract financiers for his romantic musical project.

When Chazelle was trying to recruit Emma Stone for the part of Mia in *La La Land*, he held a screening of *The Umbrellas of Cherbourg*, the legendary French musical by Jacques Demy. That perfectly explained what he was trying to do – make a musical on the streets of a city.

"It took me a little while to wrap my mind around doing a contemporary musical," says Stone. "Damien talked about Demy and how he wanted to shoot in real locations and make them look larger than life. The whole idea for *La La Land* was scary and different, and, finally, I had to say yes."

~ ~ ~

La La Land was filmed in and around Los Angeles, California. Chazelle used more than 60 locations. We won't be able to cover them all. This is not a day-long bus tour; merely a follow-the-dots glimpse at some of the key locations where the movie was shot.

Driving me around his neighborhood, my son had pointed out the blocky building at 4403 West Magnolia Boulevard which stood in for the jazz club in the movie. It's now a music studio, but you can easily do a drive-by.

As you pass, glance across the street to the other side of West Magnolia and you'll spot the retro dairy mart that's also seen in the movie.

Ryan Gosling dedicated several months to learning to play jazz piano for the film. Never learning to read music, he memorized all the finger positions on the keys. With daily practice, Gosling got good enough that he was able to perform all the piano scenes himself, without using a hand double.

Next locale to visit is the Judge Harry Pregerson Interchange. The movie's six-minute opening scene with the "Another Day of Sun" dance number in the middle of a traffic jam was filmed on the ramp that connects the carpool lanes of the 105 (Century) and 110 (Harbor) freeways. It took over two days of shooting to get the intricate choreography right. The freeway ramp was closed to regular traffic during filming, allowing the scene to be shot with cars facing towards downtown, even though in real life, traffic on that ramp heads away from downtown.

This scene sets the Technicolor tone for the film. "What's truer to L.A. than traffic?" grins Chazelle.

Your next destination just has to be Griffith Park, home of the Griffith Observatory. A planetarium scene was important to Chazelle. "I always saw the characters dancing in the stars," he says, pointing out the various spots where Mia and Sebastian celebrate falling in love through dance and song. Stone and Gosling rehearsed this dance number for three months. The Griffith Observatory is located at 2800 East Observatory Road.

The "A Lovely Night" tap dancing scene was shot on a street in Griffith Park just off Mt. Hollywood Drive. Overlooking the San Fernando Valley, the spot is officially known as Cathy's Corner.

The Lighthouse Café is the club where Sebastian explains his passion for jazz to Mia. "The music here isn't cool, smooth jazz; it's traditional – jazz as it should be, the kind Ryan Gosling's character loves," says Lighthouse manager Steven Grehl. You can find the café at 30 Pier Avenue in Hermosa Beach.

A short walk from the Lighthouse is the highly romantic Hermosa Beach Pier, where Sebastian first sings "City of Stars."

Jar is the retro-modern restaurant where early in the film Mia abandons her boyfriend, Greg (Finn Wittrock). Noted for its juicy steaks, Jar is located at 8225 Beverly Boulevard.

The El Rey Theatre is where Sebastian plays keyboards for his old friend Keith (John Legend). With its graceful art deco design by Clifford A. Balch, the El Rey used to be a cinema and a dance club before transitioning in the '90s into a music theater. Located at 5515 Wilshire Boulevard on Miracle Mile, the El Rey has been called one of "the best mid-sized venues in L.A."

The Blind Donkey at 149 Linden Avenue in Long Beach is the setting for Seb's jazz club at the end of the film – where Mia and Sebastian have their final, bittersweet encounter.

Nearby is Rose Tower, which was used as the setting for Mia's pink apartment. Located at 728 East 3rd Street in Long Beach, this 20-unit Spanish colonial complex was restored about a decade ago.

Mia and Sebastian grab some food at Sarita's Pupuseria, a Salvadoran restaurant housed (along with nearly 100 other vendors) within the downtown

Los Angeles market. Sampling the exotic food is the way to spend your visit to this site.

Later, while on their date, Mia and Seb ride the funicular Angels Flight Railway. The Railway's Top Station is located at California Plaza, 350 South Grand Avenue. It's been running since 1901. A great spot for a photo opp.

Parts of the film were shot on the Warner Bros. lot, including scenes with Mia working as a barista at a studio coffee shop. As they wander the studio's lot, Mia points out "the window that Humphrey Bogart and Ingrid Bergman looked out in *Casablanca*" – one of the film's many nods to movie history. Warner Bros is still a working studio, with 35 sound stages, 14 exterior sets, postproduction services and visitor tours. Located at 3400 West Riverside Drive in Burbank, you can take a tour for a little over $60.

Other scenes were filmed at Hollywood Center Studios, now known as Sunset Las Palmas Studios. This is an independent entertainment production lot located at 1040 North Las Palmas Avenue in Hollywood,

During the how-they-fall-in-love montage, Gosling and Stone are seen walking across the 1,500-foot-long Colorado Street Bridge that rises 150 feet above Arroyo Seco. When completed in 1913, this was the highest concrete bridge in the world, connecting Pasadena to Los Angeles.

Also, Mia and Sebastian meet at the Rialto Theatre to watch a 10 p.m. screening of *Rebel Without a Cause*. Dating back to 1925, the Rialto's façade has been described as "an odd mashup of Spanish baroque and Egyptian kitsch." A single-screen cinema that seated 1,300 people, it closed in 2007. Nonetheless, you can find the Rialto at 1023 Fair Oaks Avenue in South Pasadena.

The fictional Lipton's restaurant – where jazz purist Sebastian grudgingly agrees to play Christmas music – is really The Smokehouse, a venerable eatery frequented by actors, producers and other showbiz types. My son took us to dinner here. Located at 420 West Lakeside Drive, you can dine there too. The Smokehouse has been on this spot, across the street from the Warner Bros studio, since 1949.

~ ~ ~

Obviously, Damien Chazelle has a predilection for musical films.

He wrote the screenplay for *La La Land* in 2010, even before *Whiplash*. His idea was "to take the old musical but ground it in real life where things don't always exactly work out," and "to salute creative people who move to Los Angeles to chase their dreams."

He had his own Hollywood dreams.

"When I fell in love with musicals, I fell really hard," says Damien Chazelle.

CHAPTER 23

The Lord of the Rings Trilogy
The Hobbit Trilogy

My friend Colleen is from New Zealand. Yes, a Kiwi. Ironically, I met her in the Bahamas. And now she lives in the mountains of North Carolina.

I don't think she ever read J.R.R. Tolkien's *The Lord of the Rings* books, but I'm pretty sure she saw the movies – more for a glimpse of familiar scenery than any interest in a fantasy land called Middle-Earth.

To help Colleen out on her next trip back home, I've gone to the bother of researching where some of the key scenes from *The Lord of the Rings* Trilogy and *The Hobbit* movies were filmed.

British author John Ronald Reuel Tolkien invented a full-blown fantasy world populated not only by humans, but also by elves, dwarves, ents, hobbits, dragons, trolls, and orcs. He called it his "legendarium."

After J.R.R. Tolkien's death, his son Christopher published a series of works based on his father's extensive notes and unpublished manuscripts. These formed a connected body of stories, fictional histories, invented languages, and essays about a fantasy world called Arda and, within it, Middle-Earth.

The *Lord of the Rings* is the world's second best-selling novel of all time.

A Tolkien fan, New Zealand-based director Peter Jackson wanted to make the stories into films and pitched the idea to several studios. Following many turndowns, New Line Cinema was willing to finance a three-movie trilogy. Filming them back-to-back, Jackson gave us *The Lord of the Rings: The Fellowship of the Ring* (2001), *The Lord of the Rings: The Two Towers* (2002), and *The Lord of the Rings: The Return of the King* (2003).

Set in the fictional world of Middle-Earth, the films follow a hobbit named Frodo Baggins as he and the Company of the Ring embark on a quest to defeat the Dark Lord Sauron. The stories represent the struggle of good against evil.

The movie's ensemble cast includes Elijah Wood, Ian McKellen, Liv Tyler, Viggo Mortensen, Sean Astin, Cate Blanchett, John Rhys-Davies, Christopher Lee, Orlando Bloom, Hugo Weaving, Sean Bean, and Andy Serkis.

The three films were shot simultaneously in Jackson's native New Zealand

This was one of the most ambitious film projects ever undertaken, with a budget of $281 million (equivalent to nearly $600 million today). The gamble paid off, with it turning out to be one of the highest grossing film series of all time, raking in over $2.9 billion worldwide.

Jackson's *Lord of the Rings* films won 17 Academy Awards out of 30 nominations, including a Best Picture Oscar for *The Return of the King*.

~ ~ ~

Next, Peter Jackson made a trilogy based on Tolkien's Hobbit tales:

The Hobbit: An Unexpected Journey (2012), The Hobbit: The Desolation of Smaug (2013), and *The Hobbit: The Battle of the Five Armies (2014)*.

The series is a prequel to Jackson's *The Lord of the Rings* Trilogy.

Just to remind you, according to the Tolkien stories, a hobbit is a member of an imaginary race that's similar to humans, but smaller in size, with hairy feet.

The *Hobbit* films take place in the fictional world of Middle-Earth some sixty years before the beginning of *The Lord of the Ring*. These stories follow the hobbit named Bilbo Baggins (Martin Freeman) who at the request of the Wizard Gandalf

(Ian McKellen) agrees to accompany 13 dwarves on a quest to reclaim Lonely Mountain from the dragon Smaug (Bennedict Cumberbatch).

The ensemble cast includes James Nesbitt, Ken Stott, Evangeline Lilly, Lee Pace, and Luke Evans, with several actors reprising their roles from *The Lord of the Rings*, among them Cate Blanchett, Orlando Bloom, Ian Holm, Christopher Lee, Hugo Weaving, Elijah Wood, and Andy Serkis.

The *Hobbit* Trilogy did not fare as well with fans. Many thought it was "bloated and has no business being a trilogy." Additional material and new characters were created for the *Hobbit* films. Traditionalists objected to that, but the Hobbit material was weaker than Tokien's *The Lord of the Rings* books.

Nevertheless, Peter Jackson's *Hobbit* Trilogy became one of the highest grossing film series of all time, also bringing in $2.9 billion worldwide.

~ ~ ~

The Lord of the Rings Trilogy and *The Hobbit* Trilogy were filmed entirely in New Zealand, with locations spanning both the North and South Islands.

Here's a more detailed look at some of the key locations:

North Island:

The town of Matamata in Waikato, New Zealand, is home to the famous Hobbiton Movie Set, which served as the backdrop for the Shire. The filmmakers constructed the whole of Hobbiton, including Frodo's home Bag End, during the production of the trilogy, but took it apart after the shooting.

However, it was rebuilt for *The Hobbit* Trilogy and has remained there to this day as a popular tourist attraction.

The Hobbiton Movie Set is situated on a family-run farm about 5 miles west of Hinuera and 6.2 miles southwest of Matamata. The New Zealand Army brought in heavy equipment to construct a road to the site. The crew built the facades of 37 hobbit holes tucked into the hillside. They added gardens and hedges, a pub, a mill, and a double arch bridge. The workers also erected a 29-ton oak above Bilbo Baggins's Bag End hole, a tree that was cut down near Matamata and replanted on the site, complete with artificial leaves. The idea was to make it look like the Devonshire countryside. In Tolkien's Middle-earth, the Shire is a region reminiscent of Devonshire, England. It is described as "a bucolic, idyllic land with rolling hills and forests, much like the English countryside."

"I knew Hobbiton needed to be warm, comfortable and feel lived in," says Peter Jackson. "By letting the weeds grow through the cracks and establishing hedges and little gardens a year before filming, we ended up with an incredibly real place, not just a film set."

Matamata is a must-see if you're a *Hobbit* or *The Lord of the Rings* fan. Take a guided tour of the Hobbiton Movie Set and enjoy the town's fabulous cafés. You can visit Bag End, see the Party Tree where Bilbo celebrated his 111th birthday, and visit the Green Dragon Inn for a pint of thirst quencher. At The Shire's Rest (a café) you can dine like a Hobbit (which means a lot of food).

Half a day spent at the Hobbiton Movie Set is a highlight of Goway's The Lord of the Rings Self Drive Vacation.

Tongariro National Park – home to three active volcanoes – was used to represent Mordor, the land of Dark Lord Sauron. Mount Ngauruhoe served as the non-CGI Mount Doom.

The city of Wellington and its surrounding areas were used for various scenes, including Bree, Rivendell, and the Outer Shire. Here, you'll find the Wētā Workshop, a special effects and prop workshop where many items for the film were created. Wellington also served as the base for the film crew.

The Putangirua Pinnacles in the Aorangi Range near Wellington were used as scenes of the Outer Shire.

Kaitoke Regional Park, also near Wellington, provided the location for Rivendell, where the elf lord Elfrond lives and where Frodo recovers from his wound. You'll even find a stone gate still there that marked the entrance to Rivendell.

Found in the Waikato Region, between Hamilton and Taurango, the Hinuera Valley was served as the landscape around the Hobbiton. The dramatic rock formations of the Waitomo area are known for their glowworm caves.

The looming cliffs and unusual limestone formations at Mangaotaki Rocks near Piopio look as if they were created especially to provide the backdrop for Middle-Earth.

Mount Victoria, the highest volcanic cone on Auckland's North Shore, supplied the scenes for the hobbits leaving the Shire. Also, it was used for the Hobbiton Woods where the hobbits hide from the Ringwraiths.

And the North Island's West Coast served as the site for the Lighting of the Beacons segment.

South Island:

Queenstown provided scenes in the Dead Marshes and other locations.

Earnslaw Burn is a glacier with cascading waterfalls that tumble down a huge rock cliff. Here, Bilbo and The Company continue their quest after departing Rivendell. The area is known for the Earnshaw Burn Track, a challenging hiking trail that leads to stunning views of an icefall on Mount Earnslaw.

The stunning scenery of Fiordland National Park represents the Misty Mountains and the River Anduin. The scene where The Company flees the mountains on the backs of eagles was filmed here.

Lake Pukaki was chosen as the location for Laketown. Braemar Station at Lake Pukaki was also used for the forest slopes of Misty Mountains.

Nelson/Abel Tasman provided the backdrop for several locations, scenes like Chetwood Forest, Dimrill Dale, and the mines of Mora. Although found on private property, visitors can get a good view of the cliffs overlooking Golden Bay by signing up for a horse tour.

The picturesque town of Glenorchy served as Isengard and Lothlórien.

The Kawarau River Gorge was used to create the Gates of Argonath. Located in the Central Otago region, it's easily accessible along State Highway 6. This is where bungy jumping was invented.

Mount Sunday substituted as Edoras, the capital of Rohan. Skippers Canyon, Mavora Lakes, and Deer Park Heights also provided other Rohan locations.

~ ~ ~

Colleen and her American-born husband were talking about retiring to New Zealand. If so, I hope they can find a comfortable underground house in Hobbiton.

CHAPTER 24

James Bond Films

When I lived in the Bahamas, I frequently drove by a pink-painted oceanfront villa on the right side of the road about 2 miles west of Nassau. Its official name is Rock Point, but James Bond fans know it as Palmyra, SPECTRE villain Emilio Largo's home in the movie *Thunderball*.

The shark pool where Largo's henchman Quist becomes fish food is visible from the road. You can also see the beach area, the place where Bond shows off his skill at trap shooting. Unfortunately, being a private estate, Rock Point is not accessible to the public.

The gate is usually locked and patrolled by two very hungry looking dogs. So do not trespass.

Much damage has been done to the surrounding walls by hurricanes, and the outer pool has suffered. At one point, it was filled with sand

Once you have passed the gate, you'll come to the parking space in front of the house. This is where

Bond parked his Aston Martin DB5. The car was equipped with various gadgets, including tire slashers and oil slicks.

Next to the Rock Point entrance you will now find two 17th-Century canons, each worth over $500,000, just lying there on the grass.

Adjacent to the house is a public beach that still looks pretty much as it did in *Thunderball*.

~ ~ ~

The Commonwealth of the Bahamas consists of about 700 islands and 2,000 cays, of which only 40 or so are inhabited. They stretch over a range of 650 miles from the east coast of Florida in a south-easterly direction to the Caribbean.

Though one of the smallest islands, New Providence with the capital Nassau, is the political, economic and tourist center of the country.

Because of the subtropical climate and excellent beaches, tourism produces more than 50 per cent of the national income. It is also a popular tax haven. And a great movie location.

No fewer than seven James Bond films were (partly) shot in The Bahamas: *You Only Live Twice, Thunderball, The Spy Who Loved Me, For Your Eyes Only, Never Say Never Again, The World Is Not Enough,* and *Casino Royale.*

Almost every James Bond film with an underwater scene was filmed in the Bahamas. The producers used the crystal-clear waters around the islands to film underwater scenes for *You Only Live Twice*, the underwater car scene in *The Spy Who Loved Me*, and diving scenes in *For Your Eyes Only* – even though none of those films were set in The Bahamas.

I used to lunch at Café Martinique on Paradise Island. You'll see it in *Thunderball*. However, everything was rebuilt after Atlantis bought the island, so it's no longer recognizable. When I lived in Nassau, Paradise Island (the former Hog Island) was owned by A&P heir Huntington Hartford. Something of as playboy, he would phone my office trying to get my secretary Judy to go out with him. His yacht was anchored in Nassau Harbor. A pretty dark-haired Italian from New York, I don't think she ever accepted.

Thunderball (1965) marked the Bahamas' debut in the 007 franchise. with Nassau, Paradise Island, and the Exuma Cays serving as primary filming locations.

The fourth film in the series, Sean Connery was still taking his martinis shaken, not stirred.

Of the several *Thunderball* locations on Paradise Island, only the breakwater where Largo's scuba team assembles survives. The site is now part of the Atlantis complex.

On Paradise Beach, Bond meets the beautiful Domino, (Claudine Auger) for the first time. He engages her by pretending to have problems with his boat engine. Domino helps him out with her boat, and they come ashore on the sun-drenched tropical beach.

The waterbreaker location is easy enough to find between Cabbage beach and the resort. It's right by the lockers which you must pay to use. And if you're not a guest at the hotel you'll have to pay for a beach pass.

I used to swim off Love Beach, a lovely palm-tree-line strip of sand about 20 minutes northwest of Nassau. This is where Bond pins Vargos to a tree in *Thunderball*. However, you won't find the tree if you go look. Much of the landscape has changed due to hurricanes.

Off the coast of New Providence, an Avro Vulcan bomber which crashes into the ocean in *Thunderball* can still be visited by divers and snorkelers. Stuart Cove's Dive Bahamas runs regular trips to this site and another shipwreck from the film. Be forewarned, the plane has lost its outer skin and only the underlying structure can still be seen.

Thunderball Grotto, just west of Staniel Cay in The Exumas, is also a favorite for divers. The underwater cave system is teeming with brilliantly colored fish. At the top of the cave, a small opening permits the sun to enter and illuminate the scene. It was through this hole that Bond was rescued by helicopter. When the tide is low and the current slack, snorkelers can swim into the cave via a hidden entrance, but at high tide diving equipment is required, so proceed with caution.

~ ~ ~

Never Say Never Again (1983), while not part of the official EON Productions Bond series, stars Sean Connery in a return as James Bond. Filmed partly in Nassau, you will recognize scenes shot in downtown Nassau, along the harbor, and at other locations around the island.

The beach of the British Colonial Hotel (called the BC by locals) was where Bond meets Fatima Blush (Barbara Carrera) as she water-skis to the end of the pier and into Bond's arms. The landmark yellow building stands out in the background. The pier was especially built for the movie and the hotel kept it.

The scenes where Fatima places a bomb in Bond's room, although identified by signage as the British Colonial, was in fact filmed at the Nassau Beach Hotel. This Cable Beach property was demolished in 2012.

Also, Nigel Small-Fawcett (Rowan Atkinson) has a rendezvous with Bond in Rawson Square, recognizable by its pillared arcade. With the nearby

Straw Market, you'll find the location there on Bay Street on the island-side of the bridge.

~ ~ ~

When Daniel Craig took over as 007 with *Casino Royale* (2006) – the 21st Bond film – it was only fitting that the franchise return to its Caribbean roots with a memorable poker game scene at the Ocean Club on Paradise Island. This is where Craig made Villa 1085 a popular accommodation, where he seduced a married woman, and where he won an Aston Martin in a card game. Later, M (Dame Judi Dench) joined him here for lunch.

The resort with its terraced gardens and elegant colonial architecture became a Four Seasons property in 2017 and was renamed The Ocean Club. Visitors can check out the resort's Versailles Gardens that were also featured in the film. This hotel offers exceptional service with a four-to-one staff-to-guest ratio.

The scenes where Bond emerges from the water and romances Solange (Caterina Murino) were filmed on the beach at the Albany Resort on New Providence's south coast.

~ ~ ~

The Bahamas has stood in for other countries too.

The intense parkour scene (running, jumping, and climbing skills in an urban setting) where Bond chases Mollaka (Sébastien Foucan) at the beginning if *Casino Royal,* was set in Madagascar. But it was actually filmed at an abandoned construction site at Coral Harbour on the southside of New Providence Island.

And when Mollaka escapes to the fictitious Nambutu Embassy, the building was on the Buena Vista Estate. However, that locale has been renovated, now occupied by John Watling's Distillery.

Also, the Embassy in Madagascar is on the same block as the Distillery where the villain runs to the embassy.

The Ugandan jungle scenes in which Le Chiffre (Mads Mikkelsen) borrows $100 million dollars from a terrorist, were filmed at an abandoned property in the center of New Providence.

As for Sean Connery, the Scottish-born actor loved filming *Thunderball* and *Never Say Never Again* in the Bahamas so much that in the 1990s he bought a home in Lyford Cay (on the western tip of New Providence) and became a lunchtime regular at the One and Only Ocean Club on Paradise Island. That's where he passed away in 2020.

Connery's son Jason emailed me to tell me of his father's death. I had a vodka martini in Memoriam – shaken, not stirred.

However, in real life, Sean Connery preferred red wine, usually a Merlot.

CHAPTER 25
The African Queen

Yes, I have a replica of the Maltese Falcon sitting on my bookshelf. It reminds me of one of my favorite Humphrey Bogart films. I'm a big fan of Bogie movies – *The Maltese Falcon, Casablanca, To Have and Have Not, The African Queen*.

Before his breakthrough in the noirish film *High Sierra* (1941), Humphrey DeForest Bogart had appeared in supporting roles for more than a decade, regularly portraying gangsters. However, Bogart was "catapulted to stardom" as Sam Spade, the private detective in John Huston's *The Maltese Falcon* (1941).

In 1999, the American Film Institute selected Humphrey Bogart as the greatest male star of classic American cinema.

Bogie had wonderful co-stars – dewy-eyed Ingrid Bergman in *Casablanca*; his future wife, husky-voiced Lauren Bacall in *To Have and Have Not*; and a crusty Katharine Hepburn in *The African Queen*.

I used to pass Kate Hepburn sweeping her townhouse's sidewalk at 244 East 49th Street in New York. My co-op was about three blocks away.

And I often bumped into Lauren Bacall at the Amagansett Market on Long Island. I almost bought a house next door to her out there in the Hamptons.

Bacall had been a 19-year-old ingenue when she fell for 44-year-old Bogart. He divorced his third wife to marry Bacall during their second movie together, *The Big Sleep* (1946).

Bogart led the original Hollywood Rat Pack. Bacall gave the group its name. Errol Flynn, Nat King Cole, Mickey Rooney, David Niven, Judy Garland, Frank Sinatra, and others hung out at the home of Bogie and Bacall. After Bogart died, Sinatra took over leadership, coalescing the group to him, Dean Martin, Sammy Davis Jr., Joey Bishop, and (until a falling out) Peter Lawford.

~ ~ ~

The African Queen (1951) gave Bogart his only Oscar. The adventure film was based on the same-named 1935 novel by C.S. Forester. Directed by John Houston, it stars Bogart and Katharine Hepburn as a boat pilot and a traveling missionary going down the Ulanga River in German East Africa.

The movie was filmed on a tributary of the Congo River, including the Ruiki River in the Democratic Republic of the Congo, which stood in for the Ulanga in the film. The filming also took place on the Nile in Murchison Falls National Park in Uganda.

Shooting on location was unusual for the time, given that a Technicolor camera was large and cumbersome, not east to transport in a jungle setting. It's said director John Huston decided to go on location in Africa so he could hunt elephants between takes.

Visiting these locations where *The African Queen* was filmed is difficult.

The best you can do is take a boat trip: The German gunboat *Königin Luise* in the film was inspired by the *Gaf Goetzen*, a World War I vessel which was sunk in 1916 during the Battle of Lake Tanganyika. However, the British refloated the *Graf Goetzen* in 1924 and placed her in service on Lake Tanganyika in 1927 as a passenger ferry. Operated by the Marine Services Company Ltd. of Tanzania, you can catch a ride on the *MV Liemba* (as she is now called). The ferry sails between the ports of Kigoma, Tanzania, and Mpulunga in Zambia.

The other half of the film was shot in the UK, particularly the scenes in which Bogart and Hepburn are seen in the water. These were shot in water tanks at Worton Hall Studios in Isleworth, just outside of London.

The shots of German-occupied Fort Shona were also filmed at Worton Hall, where a fortress set was constructed. But that's long since been dismantled.

Visiting Worton Hall is problematic. The studios closed in 1952 and has been converted into 220-square-foot apartments for high-profile artists and creative industries (now known as the Worton Hall Industrial Estate). Also, part of the building is used as the Isleworth driving test center. The sound stages and water tanks are gone.

Best you can do is observe London's population of feral ring-necked parakeets, said to be progeny of birds that escaped during the filming of *The African Queen*.

~ ~ ~

What about the *African Queen* itself? Originally known as the *S/L Livingstone*, the 30-foot steamboat was built in England by Lytham Shipbuilding and Engineering Company and used by the British East Africa Railway Company to transport cargo and passengers on the Ruki River and across Lake Albert.

The *African Queen* wasn't really blown up like you see in the movie. The boat was found in Cairo, Egypt, in the 1970s, with coal still in its bilges. Purchased and shipped to the United States, she has had a succession of owners, including actor Fess Parker (TV's *Davy Crockett*).

The boat was restored in April 2012 and is now on display as a tourist attraction in Key Largo, Florida.

Footnote: No, Bogie's classic film *Key Largo* (1948) was not filmed in Key Largo. In *Hollywood's Golden Age*, Chris Whiteley tells us:

"The film was shot primarily at the Warner Bros. Studios, Burbank, in order to keep costs down. The beach and hotel exterior were constructed on the Warner Bros. backlot; the interior scenes were filmed on a sound stage; and the boat scenes were filmed in Sound Stage 21, a huge indoor water tank. Exterior shots of the hurricane were taken from stock footage used in *Night Unto Night*, a Ronald Reagan melodrama which Warner Bros. also produced in 1948. Filming took 78 days."

~ ~ ~

Actually, there two *African Queen* boats used in the movie. The first boat was filmed in the Belgian Congo on a tributary of the Congo River; the second boat was filmed on the Nile in Murchison Falls National Park in Uganda.

This second *African Queen* was built in 1950 for the movie. What was left of the vessel was discovered by Yank Evans, a Patagonian mechanical engineer, while working on the roads in Murchison Falls National Park in 1984. He asked the locals what it was, and they said, "Well, that's the *African Queen*. He bought the steel hull from the National Parks for $1.

After restoring the boat, Evans took her to Kenya when he moved there in 1997. The *African Queen*'s new home became a trailer in his garden.

Cam McLeay, a Kiwi who lived in Uganda with his family, purchased the Nile *African Queen* after hearing her amazing story. "I said you're joking, and he said no, as far as I know she's still on a trailer in Nairobi," recalled McLeay. "I just called up a mobile phone number and he said yeah she's still on the trailer, come and have a look!"

"He wanted to sell it, but I think he was just so connected to the boat. Restoring her was a labor of love, really," said McLeay.

Cam McLeay's plan was to offer tours on the Nile in this steam-powered *African Queen* from his Wildwaters Lodge in Uganda.

You can go to Wildwaters if you're adventurous. The lodge is found on Kalagala Island, on the River Nile just downstream from Jinga. It's only reachable by boat.

For me, Key Largo is a lot closer than East Africa, so I stopped off at MM100 to check out the Belgian Congo's *African Queen*. The historic steamboat is docked at Marna Del Mar, a part of the Holiday Inn Complex in Key Largo, the northernmost island in the Florida Keys.

It was right there, moored to the narrow wooden dock. You could almost imagine Charlie Allnutt bragging, "Nobody in Africa, but yours truly, can get a good head of steam on the old *African Queen*."

I didn't go for a cruise, but the guy at the dock graciously let me step on board. For a moment, just a moment, I felt like I was steaming down the Ulanga with Charlie and Rose in *The African Queen*.

CHAPTER 26
The Rose Tattoo

My wife and lived in Key West for over 20 years. Our home – a classic Temple Revival style two-story house replete with gingerbread – was only a few blocks from Tennessee Williams' little cottage on tree-shrouded Duncan Street.

Known as one of the 20th Century's greatest American playwrights, Thomas Lanier Williams III – Tennessee to the audiences of his plays – lived in Key West from 1949 until his death in 1983. He first visited the island in 1941, returning frequently until he settled there more or less permanently.

His sister Rose lived in a house he bought for her on nearby Von Phister Street. Having had a lobotomy in her teens, Rose Williams required a companion, my friend Lynda Hambright.

"Key West had in those days a very authentic frontier atmosphere which was delightful," Williams said. "It's the only place in this country where it's warm enough for me to swim every day of the year. The sky is always so clear, and the water's so blue."

During those 34 years, he wrote many award-winning plays – "The Glass Menagerie," "A Streetcar Named Desire," "Cat on a Hot Tin Roof," "The Rose Tattoo," "Orpheus Descending," "Sweet Bird of Youth," "Summer and Smoke," and "The Night of the Iguana."

His sister Rose served as his muse.

"The Glass Menagerie" is about a young man named Tom who guiltily leaves his disabled sister behind with their overbearing Southern Belle mother. The sister's nickname is "Blue Roses."

Art imitates life, as they say.

Further evidence: "The Rose Tattoo" directly evokes his sister's name.

~ ~ ~

The Rose Tattoo (1955) was based on Tennessee Williams' Broadway play. Directed by Daniel Mann (*Come Back, Little Sheba*; *The Teahouse of the August Moon*), the film starred Anna Magnini and Burt Lancaster.

In the movie, Magnani plays Serafina Delle Rose, an Italian seamstress whose husband has been killed in a truck crash. Three years later, she's still deep in grief, but comes back to life when she meets another goodlooking Italian truck driver, played by Burt Lancaster.

Tennessee Williams was a good friend of Anna Magnini. Although the Italian actress was relatively unknown in America, Williams had written "The Rose Tattoo" with her in mind. But Magnini declines the role because of her poor English, so Maureen Stapleton had starred in the Broadway play.

The play being successful on Broadway, Hal Wallis bought the film rights.

When it came time to do the film version, Magnani's English had improved. It would be her first English-speaking role in a Hollywood film.

Magnani won an Academy Award for Best Actress. She was the first Italian actress to win an Oscar. The film also won Oscars for Best Art Direction and Best Cinematography. It received five other nominations, including Best Picture.

Although the play was set in a small Mississippi Gulf town, much of the film was shot on location in Key West. The setting is not specifically mentioned in the film.

The Rose Tattoo was filmed in Key West because the filmmakers, while scouting locations, found a perfect fit for the exterior of the house owned by Serafina Delle Rose on Duncan Street, which became known as the "Rose Tattoo House." Located at 1421 Duncan Street, it became the focal point for exterior shots of the film. The actors often used Tennessee Williams' house next door for costume changes.

The film production spent about a month shooting in Key West. Many locals appeared as extras in the film. Paul Toppino said his whole family was in the movie because they're Italian. He was 12 when the movie was made and even has a line in the very first scene.

> Paul and another boy are following the woman who is sleeping with Serafina's husband. When she comes out of a tattoo parlor, she tells them she got a rose tattoo.
> "Where did they put it on you?" he asks the woman.
> "Right over my heart, little boy," she answers.

Years later, Tennessee Williams had an enormous Mosaic of a rose tattoo embedded in the floor of the pool behind his house. It's still there.

~ ~ ~

For visitors, Key West has lots of points of interest – from the Hemingway Home to the newly restored Elizabeth Bishop House, from the Customs House Museum to the Key West Lighthouse. If you want to retrace the film locations for *The Rose Tattoo*, that's easy to do also.

In fact, you can see them all by bicycle. There are plenty bicycles and motor scooters for rent on this touristy island. The total land area of Key West is only 4.2 square miles.

To orient yourself, start off with a visit to the Tennessee Williams Exhibit, a small museum at 513 Truman Avenue. There you will find an extensive collection of photographs, first edition plays and books, a typewriter used by the author while writing in Key West, videos, even a scale model of his Duncan Street cottage. You can even see the stairs that was the site of a romantic exchange between Rosa and Jack (Marisa Pavan and Ben Cooper) in the movie. At the time of the filming, the stairs were part of the property of Key West High School.

Next, you will want to cycle past Tennessee Williams' house at 1431 Duncan Street. He called it his "Tom Thumb Cottage" because of its "petite size and magical, tucked-away charm, so removed from the hustle and bustle of the mainstream."

Conveniently, the "Rose Tattoo House" is located right next door, on the corner of Pearl and Duncan. "The location scout didn't even know that Tennessee Williams lived next door," says the current owner. "But it was just right for what they were looking for." The house has been restored – right down to the bedroom wallpaper – as an Airbnb. Yes, you could stay there.

Then, you should peddle over to 915 Von Phister to view the house where his sister Rose lived. Despite Rose's lobotomy, she loved to paint and to swim in the pool behind her home. She frequently accompanied her brother to dinner, able to converse in a rudimentary manner. He was devoted to her.

In the movie's Mardi Gras Club scene, a few familiar faces appear among the extras as Serafina storms by the men on bar stools. Tennessee Williams can be seen in a striped shirt at the bar and the shorter man in the white suit helping restrain Serafina is Frank Merlo, Tennessee Williams longtime companion. This was filmed at a location on the east side of Duval Street, north of Front Street, where the CVS pharmacy is now located (formerly 92 Duval Street).

The church where Serafina meets with her priest is the Basila of St. Mary, Star of the Sea. Still open to worshipers, you will find it at 1010 Windsor Lane. The magnificent cathedral faces Truman Avenue. And while you're there, stop to light a candle at the adjacent Our Lady of Lourdes Grotto, built in 1922 by nuns to ward off hurricanes.

Another stop: Tennessee Williams wrote the final draft of "A Streetcar Named Desire" in 1947 while staying at the La Concha Hotel. You can visit the historic hotel at 430 Duval Street, the town's main drag. It's the tallest building on the island.

Sure, some scenes were filmed back in Hollywood at Paramount Studios (5555 Melrose Avenue), but those sets are long gone.

~ ~ ~

In March, there's a month-long birthday celebration in Key West for the Tennessee Williams, complete with film screenings, plays, art, and poetry readings. Recently, Richard Thomas (TV's "The Waltons") performed a one-man show, reading from the letters of Tennessee Williams.

While living in Key West, I served several years as the president of the Key West Art & Historical Society, overseeing four museums. One of them was the Tennessee Williams Exhibition. I have a photo of me standing next to the large cardboard cutout of the playwright that greets people at the door.

ACKNOWLEDGMENTS

While I have personally traveled to all the places in this book (an exception being New Zealand), much of the information here is an aggregation of numerous sources. The Internet is a wonderful tool when researching backgrounds of places visited, histories, people, or specific details. My personal thanks to any I have cribbed from in order to present a more complete picture of an interesting locale.

Movie history is both learned from books and articles and websites, as well as from watching the movies themselves. I have watched the movies covered in this book multiple times. In fact, writing *Dirty Dancing in an Ice Storm with the X-Men* was a good excuse to watch many of them again.

You should watch ach of the movies before visiting any related filming sites. That way, you can compare the actual location with the celluloid scene with a fresh memory.

Enjoy!

Shirrel Rhoades
Lake Lure,
North Carolina

ABOUT THE AUTHOR

SHIRREL RHOADES is not only a travel writer, but he's also a syndicated movie critic with his reviews appearing in a dozen or so newspapers of the Adams Publishing Group. Previously, he has been the film critic for *The Florida Times Union*, Cooke Communications, and Cox Media Group. His Hollywood profiles have appeared in *Good Old Days* and other publications. His travel articles have appeared in *The Bahamas Handbook*, *Cayman Island Holiday Guide*, and *The Saturday Evening Post*, among other venues. He has written numerous travel books, including the titles (seven so far) in this *You Can Go There* series.

Rhoades has also been a publisher, feature writer, college professor, museum president, and filmmaker. He and his wife Diane currently live in the mountains of North Carolina with their two dogs, three cats, and Venus flytrap.

AbsolutelyAmazingEbooks.com or
AA-eBooks.com

Thank you for reading.
Please review this book. Reviews
help others find Absolutely Amazing eBooks and
inspire us to keep providing these marvelous tales.
If you would like to be put on our email list
to receive updates on new releases,
contests, and promotions, please go to
AbsolutelyAmazingEbooks.com and sign up.

For sales, editorial information, subsidiary rights information
or a catalog, please write or phone or e-mail

AbsolutelyAmazingBooks
Manhanset House
Shelter Island Hts., New York 11965, US
Tel: 212-427-7139
www.BrickTowerPress.com
bricktower@aol.com
www.IngramContent.com

www.ingramcontent.com/pod-product-compliance
Lightning Source LLC
Chambersburg PA
CBHW070612170426
43200CB00012B/2669